CANYONLANDS

BY

JOSHUA HODGE

CANYONLANDS

My adventures in the National Parks and the beautiful wild

BY JOSHUA HODGE

Names: Joshua Hodge, author
Title: Canyonlands: My adventures in the National Parks and the beautiful wild
Subjects: National Parks, Travel, Memoir

Cover and interior design by Joshua Hodge
Cover photo by Dom David

More information available at www.joshhodge.com

First Edition
Trade Paperback

Published by Joshua Hodge

Printed in the United States of America

Contents

"Life is a great adventure...accept it in such a spirit"

- Theodore Roosevelt

Introduction

I close my eyes and take a breath. I see a mule deer pause and turn its head towards me. We lock eyes, and for a moment we share something. Life, we both have it, and we both need it. Then it leaves, dancing off into the forest. The ghostly white aspens of the forest are gradually replaced with the warm red rock of Utah where a lizard scurries off quickly and a golden mantle ground squirrel pauses for a picture. As I kneel down with my camera, I feel the hot summer sun grabbing my shoulders. When I look up from my camera, the landscape is replaced by beautiful majestic mountains covered in pines and alpine tundra. Sun beams shoot down from the cracks in the capstone clouds. Snow paints the tops of the mountains in the distance, but in front of me a marmot whimsically flops around next to a stoic old mountain goat. They are very different creatures sharing this same patch of tundra. I look at this and ponder, what does it mean? Could it be that nothing is wasted, that these scenes and experiences in nature are orchestrated to speak to us? I turn around and the majestic mountains are replaced by the rocks of a canyon rim, and right in front of me I see two chipmunks race around in a game of tag. Then my eyes are lifted to the distance where a series of deep dark cavities wear away at the earth. They present themselves in a thousand shades of color, endless, mysterious. *What do these say about life?* I ask myself. These are the Canyonlands and they are full of meaning and help us rediscover ourselves.

It was 2016, the year of the National Park Service's centennial. I was twenty-six years old. As a elementary school teacher I was off work for the summer and was embarking on a month long camping road trip through the great American Southwest. On a lifelong quest to visit all sixty one U.S. National Parks, this summer I would check eleven off my list. I was excited to take in all the views, hike many trails, lose myself in the wild, and capture many photos.

This trip was not the beginning of my National Park quest nor my romance with the natural world. My first visit to a National Park was to Acadia National Park as a young child. My family had moved from its roots in northern Illinois to Massachusetts, and a few times my family would vacation from Massachusetts to the coast of Maine. My parents very much enjoyed the rocky cliffs which spilled into the ocean, the forest covered hills, the ponds, lighthouses, sandy beaches, buttery lobster, and quaint harbor towns.

When my family moved from Chicago to Massachusetts we lived in several houses, and there always was a forest in the backyard. As a child, my brothers and I would spend quite a bit of free time playing out in the woods, patching forts built out of fallen limbs, running around pretending, racing sticks in the creek, or simply exploring. We also had a nearby state park, forest preserves, and beaches we would visit regularly. An appreciation and respect for the natural world began when I was young, but it was never a focus, a passion, nor the wonderland it is for me today. As I grew and experienced hardships, through failing health and ambition, the forest became a place of peace and comfort— a place to restore my soul and rediscover myself.

At age twenty-three, after moving to Kentucky, I took the couple hour drive down into east Tennessee during my fall break and fell in love with the Great Smoky Mountains National Park, a park extremely rich in life and brimming with stories and legends from the native Cherokees to the early Appalachian settlers. It's a beautiful, mysterious treasure cove of life and culture. This park experience led me on a trail and addictive quest to see America and soak up the richness of the National Parks. My next National Park experi-

ence would be a trip in the summer of 2015 from Death
Valley into Yosemite and Sequoia, over to the California
coast and the Channel Islands, looping around back to Joshua Tree, the Grand Canyon, and Zion.

Back home in Kentucky, with a new love for the National Parks, during the school year I would get involved
with the National Park Service in the Big South Fork National River and Recreation Area, adopting a trail in the
Cumberlands of old coal country and officially serving as a
Trail Keeper. Volunteering with the National Park Service
really helped me take ownership of the parks, learning about
their structure, inner-workings, and their importance to so
many people. We are truly fortunate to have these places as
shared lands.

Now, with strength and ambition restored, the National Parks have become not only a place to seek further
restoration but also a source of inspiration and a place to put
myself up to physical challenges. The mountains reached and
the terrains explored instill in me a greater confidence in myself and my abilities.

During my 2016 National Park adventure, which this
book explores, I would come to discover that the deepness
of the Canyonlands and the highest of the mountain peaks,
and everything that grows and roams in-between, would
hold incredible symbolic meaning and significance. I would
come to discover and truly believe that all of the natural
world is intentionally designed with rich meaning and sym-
bolism to guide us to spiritual truths, and that it all connects
back to ourselves and points us to God who is the author of
all beauty.

Among those who read this book there may be various views on what the nature of this book is. For some they
will read this book and ponder these moments of inspiration
and explore them further in their own lives. Others may
glide over them and find this book as more of a how-to

guide to execute camping trips in the Southwest. They may take from this book ideas on what to do in specific parks, considering my recommendations on hiking trails and sites to see. Another group of people who read this book are the people who long for adventure but for whatever reasons cannot get out and visit these places, and so they will use this book as a means of escape, a way to travel alongside me on these adventures.

If this book fails to be any of these things for the reader, at its most rudimentary essence I see my book as a piece of historical documentation. It documents what it was like at the mark of the National Park Service's centennial to visit these places. Not only does it capture these parks in a specific and monumental moment in park history but it also shows what it is like to travel freely in the United States in the early twenty-first century, and it captures the unique perspective of a solo young man's journey at such a time.

This book came about after having come back from this trip full of stories of adventure and inspiration to share. I began writing these episodes down in an internet blog. When I realized people were interested in what I was saying, and I was developing a following, I concluded it was fitting to share it all in its most complete form, gathering up my blog entries, adding to them, holding nothing back, and creating this book. Doing so was a pleasure, as I got to re-explore these places and relive the adventures through recollection.

Except for one chapter, "The Canyons in My Life," the cornerstone of this work, everything in this book is written retrospectively, reflecting back over six months to a year to retell my adventures. I also relied on itineraries, maps, photos, and journal notes to construct these accounts with the greatest accuracy possible. I retell what I learned and what I perceived, but writing this book did not involve research into the parks. It is solely based on experience and my own perceptions. By indulging in such things, and relying heavily on memory, there may be moments in this book in which my recollection differs from that which is fundamentally true. I hope that if such an instance occurs that you pardon the author and remember the nature of this work.

Above all, I hope as you read this book, you take it as an adventure and enjoy the journey. I hope you can see the mountain tops, observe the aspen rattle, smell the sweet pines, and feel the snowy hillside slide under your feet. This book is intended to be read slowly, carefully, chronologically, and in quiet. If at any time you wish my descriptions of certain vistas or locations were explored further, it is in those moments that you pause, employ your imagination, and visualize the scenery in your mind. Let this book be a guide to take you further into the wild, to explore your imagination, because just as vast is the wilderness around us, so too is the wilderness of the imagination that lies within you.

With all of this said, welcome to my adventure. Trust me as your guide. We begin our journey on flight 2030 from Chicago Midway International Airport to Arizona. Brace yourself for heat as we will step out of Phoenix Sky Harbor into the arid 104 degrees on the last day of May.

FREE AND WILD

"By yourself?" they always ask, as if the thought of camping and exploring by oneself is incomprehensible.

"Yes, by myself," I reply.

"What about bears?" they ask.

Bears are awesome. Such strength. I respect the bear. I know that my adventures out in the wild and in the National Parks by myself are not very common, but I have never felt among danger in the parks. To me they are safe places, beautiful sanctuaries, removed from the troubles of human society where the greatest danger to man is the fellow man. Here in the bliss of the wild, wrapped among ponderosa pines, hidden in grand canyons and peaceful deserts, with the company of the rushing river and solace of the moon, gazing at majestic mountains and stretching prairies, here I am at home. Here I find myself closer to the perfection of God. The wilderness has never felt dangerous to me, but to me it is the safest place I can be. It's a place of healing where the creator himself locks eyes with his creation and speaks to me.

Alone in the wild has never brought loneliness, because alone in the wild is to truly be in the company of many– the whispering trees, the roaring waters, the howling, the singing, the calling. All together they form an orchestra with one voice pointing me to and drawing me back to the source of all life. Theodore Roosevelt, one of my most admired adventurers said, "The farther one gets into the wilderness, the greater is the attraction of its lonely freedom." Freedom waits there to be found in the wilderness, and once you find it you are free– free to run up mountain sides, slide into ravines, stroll through deserts, venture through caves, admire crashing waves, and ponder canyon depths.

So a better question than "by yourself?" would be "free and wild?" and yes, I would reply, "free and wild."

The National Park system consists of 59 official National Parks, but over 400 park units, which means in addition to those parks which bear the simple title of "National Park" there are also National Historic Parks, National Recreation Areas, National Rivers, Seashores, Lakeshores and simply an extensive gamut of sites managed by the National Park Service. It is my goal to visit the core 61 National Parks and visit as many other sites I can along the way. As of now I have visited forty National Parks and because my experiences within these parks has been so extensive, I have decided now is the time to share with you all that I have seen and experienced. In these parks not only can I recount for you many intriguing real life adventures, but I can also share with you my musings and moments of inspiration, all the internal things I found in these places. Because just as great is the wilderness around me, so too my mind is a great wilderness. The living landscape and the beauty of the physical wilderness around me illuminates and inspires that which grows wild within me.

She sat next to me on the airplane repeatedly puckering her lips and taking selfies with her phone. She had to be somewhere in her twenties. She took out her makeup, then attempted to tweak her image. "So where are you going?" she asked. I shared with her my plans to visit thirteen National Parks this summer.

"By yourself?" she questioned me.

"Yes, by myself."

"In a tent?" she asked, after I shared my camping plans. "You cannot camp in a tent out West. All the snakes and scorpions will get inside while you are sleeping. You have to sleep in a hammock." I was unphased by her remarks. I knew better.

"I'm not worried. I was out West last summer and only encountered a rattlesnake once on a trail. It was no big deal."

"I'm not scared of rattlesnakes either. I used to pick them up and play with them back home in Tennessee when I was a kid," she explained. I was not convinced.

"What are your plans?" I inquired.

"First off I'm going to relax by my friend's pool in Phoenix." Those were not her exact words, for her words were much more vulgar. I don't know why she had to make amiable conversation into something so repulsive. She then proceeded to tell me of her plans to backpack with her friends into the Grand Canyon and stay two nights.

"Do you know how much water I should bring?" She inquired, then proceeded with, "…I mean, I have a couple of water bottles."

I'm thinking to myself, *You're telling me it's too dangerous to sleep in a tent in the desert, yet you are the one who is entertaining the thought that maybe two water bottles will be enough for a two night backpacking trip into the Grand Canyon.*

"You're going to need about a liter or two every hour. You are going to need gallons of water and you should carry a water filter," I informed. "You can never have too much water in the desert."

As she continued to take more pucker-faced selfies I thought to myself this is a prime example of what I hope to get away from on this trip– the vulgar and self absorbed. *This girl's friends are going to have to carry her out of the Grand Canyon*, I thought. *I sure hope her friends know what they are doing.*

I stepped out of Phoenix Sky-Harbor into the blistering heat, which to me felt great. The warmth of the desert in the summertime is such an embracing comforting feel. However, I ran out of space when packing my suitcase, so I was wearing layers and was first burning up before I could enjoyed the dry heat blowing across my skin. My first task was checking out my rental car. I was able to secure a whole month for $600. I chose the Hyundai Accent, because it's what I drive, and I know it has super great gas milage and is a tough little vehicle. After renting one the previous summer and taking it backcountry on dirt roads in Death Valley and having it climb up to summits in the Sierra Nevada, I knew it was the vehicle I wanted to partner with for a while. My first stop with my vehicle was at a Chipotle, to load up on some calories for the adventure ahead. Here in the parking lot I was able to finally shed layers and feel a less suffocating Arizona welcome. Next, I went to Walmart to stock up on water, an essential move. Then finally with great anticipation I was off to my first truly notable destination– Saguaro National Park.

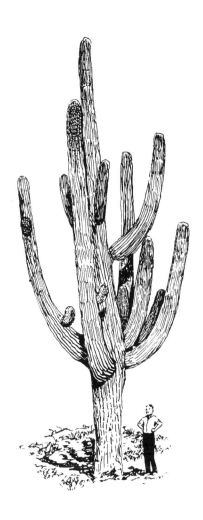

SAGUARO: LAND OF THE KILLER BEES

The Africanized Honey Bees, a.k.a. "killer bees," are found throughout Saguaro National Park. What makes them so dangerous is that even if you offend one bee, the insect releases a pheromone that attracts the rest of the colony in a swarm to assault the perpetrator, or so I've read. And if you end up finding yourself too close to a hive in the bees sacred "safe space," you might as well consider yourself dead.

These bees are no joke. They are a cross-breed that were mixed to increase honey production in Brazil but later made their way into south Texas and now southern Arizona. I was reading all about the Africanized Honey Bee after seeing the safety warning on the Saguaro National Park website.

Needless to say, I had no encounters with bees at Saguaro National Park. Everything about my time in the park was pleasant. It started at the Red Hills Visitor Center at the Saguaro West Tucson Mountain District. Something a bit peculiar about this National Park is that there are two distinct parts of the park separated by the city of Tucson.

When I got out of my car at the visitor center I noticed the National Park centennial flag flying high, a beautiful vista of Saguaro cacti all around me, and the mountains resting in the distance. Inside a park ranger, or perhaps just a visitor center employee, told me hiking is not recommended in the heat but that I could drive the Bajada Scenic Loop. I appreciated the advice, but I knew she didn't know that last summer I went hiking and camping in Death Valley. I can handle the heat. While I had her attention I asked for the best directions to get to my campground at Catalina State Park. She was very friendly and helpful, giving me area maps and detailed directions. I have only ever had very positive experiences with everyone who works for the National Park Service. As tradition, before leaving the visitor center I purchased a pin. I purchase a pin at every National Park I visit. It's my one cost effective souvenir.

After simply taking some pictures outside and around the visitor center I drove to the Desert Discovery Nature Trail, which is a short interpretive half-mile loop around various cacti. There were some impressive Saguaros to observe. I learned that the inside of the Saguaro cactus can be up to twenty degrees cooler than the air outside. Therefore birds, kangaroo rats, and even foxes find shelter within the cactus. I would never have known this and find it fascinating that there is much more to the cactus than meets the eye. Walking around the trail loop was intriguing, as simple and short as it was. I had been in deserts before but not a desert with so much cacti and plants. The ground itself was very barren and crusty, but all over, and placed, in such an impressive array were all sort of cacti and rocks. It almost looked like it was designed purposely despite it being wild. Also looking up at the Saguaro evoked a feeling similar to that of looking upon the mighty Sequoia— both are iconic, stately, and extremely resilient plants. While the Sequoia is largely fire resistant, the Saguaro is heat and sun resistant, enduring extreme heat and sunlight. These plants just give off an inspiring essence of strength.

Here on the nature trail I took quite a few photos, not only of cacti and the mountains over to one side, but admittedly of myself. I wanted to get a picture of myself with the Saguaro. I have a walking stick that also doubles as a monopod for my camera. In many terrains it's easy to

shove the stick into the ground and set the timer on my camera. Here the desert floor was so hard I could not get my stick to stand upright, so taking photos was a bit more challenging.

There were many small lizards scurrying about this trail too. I did manage to get a few good lizard pictures.

After my peaceful trail walk I embarked on the one-way Bajada Scenic Loop in my car. Since it is one-way it was a commitment. There was no turning around- although at times I was concerned it was a little too rough on the car. But I managed without any problem at all. I pulled over at a few times to take pictures and took a short hike up Signal Hill to check out some petroglyphs– the first of many petroglyphs I would see on this trip.

I knew my time in Saguaro National Park would be brief. I wasn't planning extensive hikes. I wasn't planning to stay long. I mean after all, killer bees! But in all sincerity, I knew it was a small National Park. So after a couple hours I was done. That was it. I left just thinking that it was very pleasant and something new. I had never experienced this type of desert landscape and had never seen the Saguaro in its natural habitat.

I departed Saguaro National Park and made my way around the outskirts of Tucson to Catalina State Park where I had reserved a campsite in advance. When I made my reservation I did so online rather blindly. When I arrived I was surprised to find that my reserved campsite was probably the most scenic one in the whole place. From where I pitched my tent I had an amazing view of the Catalina

Mountains, which were golden with the warm glow of late evening sun resting upon them. There were a number of holes in the ground where rather large ants and beetles would run in and out. I tried setting up my tent in the least obtrusive area. While I was setting up my tent I saw a coyote trotting around just next to my campsite with the mountains behind him.

This campground was not remote. It was close to the entrance of the park and had newly laid blacktop all throughout. It was well developed, with trash receptacles and bathrooms with showers. However, I only saw one other campsite occupied, so I was pretty much alone. It was very peaceful.

I pitched my Kelty Salida 2, my new tent, one of two tents I brought on this trip. Kelty is very airy and intended for hot desert environments, while my other tent, more sturdy and insulated, which I call "True Blue," is for colder and wetter environments.

After I set up camp I drove across the street from the state park to none other than Walmart– very convenient. Now, camping in a park across the street from a Walmart in say Kentucky sounds just very sketchy. But this Walmart had to be the nicest fanciest Walmart I have ever been to. The parking lot was immaculate with landscaped islands and classical music piped throughout. It did seem very fitting though, because surrounding this area were private planned communities with very fancy and expensive desert oases.

I bought a sandwich, Greek yogurt, and an apple, which I later ate in my car for dinner as well as food for the next couple days. I also had to buy lot of gear for the month ahead. Since I arrived to the West by plane I could only bring so much, so I had to buy a sleeping bag, pillow, matches, batteries, and food storage containers. I also bough an $8 camping air mattress for those nights I would really need a good sleep.

This night I slept in my tent on the ground in just my sleeping bag. I brought my road atlas and driving GPS with me into the tent to work on my route for the following day. I wasn't looking at the atlas very long before I fell asleep. I slept well, except remembering waking up a few times cold. I wasn't expecting it to get cold at night. In the early morning I woke up to a chorus of coyotes. Later I took advantage of the shower at the campground, knowing my next opportunity for a shower would be a number of days away, a few National Parks later, and on the other side of the Navajo Nation.

I got in my car ready to slide up the east side of Arizona to Petrified Forest National Park. Here I would secure my first wilderness permit and backpack into the wilderness to spend the night.

BECOMING "ONE" WITH NATURE

As I approached Petrified Forest National Park I started playing one of the Star Wars soundtracks. I was half expecting to find an Imperial craft flying above me, a Lothal cat roaming the landscape, or an inquisitor with a bright red lightsaber emerging onto the scene. When I had seen pictures of this park it reminded me entirely of the planet Lothal from *Star Wars: Rebels*. Lothal is the home planet of Ezra Bridger, and a unique landscape with a combination of prairie and desert with striped and rounded rock formations standing solitarily in fields.

When I am planning my National Park adventures I do plan for the music that is going to accompany my arrival at each park. Last year I chose the *Planes: Fire and Rescue* soundtrack for driving into Yosemite, because I learned the creators of the movie were inspired by the park. The soundtrack accompanied the park just perfectly, and now when I play the music from *Planes: Fire and Rescue* images, memories,

and feelings from Yosemite come back to me very vividly.
Music in very powerful and a place in which to store memories.

Before arriving at the Petrified Forest, I traveled
from Saguaro National Park and was captivated by the scenic drive to get there. I arrived via highways 77 and 60
which passed through the Tonto National Forest ("tonto" is
the Spanish word for stupid– maybe not the best word
choice). I also passed through the San Carlos and White
Mountain Apache Tribe Reservations. I pulled over maybe
five times to snap pictures and take it all in. The roads were
curving around the edge of striking canyons and over majestic mountains. The views were just so stunning that at one
particular spot I pulled my car over to the side of the road,
stepped outside to the embracing heat, and just sat on the
edge of the canyon overlooking the bend of a river and
wept.

I cried. I cried in response to the beauty of it all. I
had probably seen more beautiful vistas, but not for a long
while, so this cut deep inside me. I also felt a sense of accomplishment in being able to arrive at such a beautiful and
new vista. Being able to take these adventures is not easy. It
follows a year of hard work. It follows a year of trying to
take six-hundred students from point A to point B in the
classroom. It follows a semester of grad school when I'm
expected to work more hours than what exists. It follows
my annual battle with my health insurance company which
would rather have me dead. My summer vacation marks the
end of all of these things. It's a checkpoint and an oppor-

tunity to look back and see that I survived. It's a moment to really stop and take in the finish line and release all the emotions that have been suppressed to stay afloat. It's a moment to realize I don't have any responsibilities, except to breath deeply.

It's also in these beautiful vistas that I see a reflection. I see a reflection of God. I don't see happenstance and chaos that create a beautiful vista but I see something carefully designed, placed, and molded with time and weather by the Creator. And in such moments as this one, when I stop to really take in the beauty, it's as if I lock eyes with the Creator. God is showing me something incredible he has created. As I am captivated in awe by the work of art around me, I realize the very same Artist who constructs these amazing views with great depths, great heights, and abundant detail, is the same One who created and molded me. I'm overcome with thankfulness and humility as I am reminded where I come from. I come from the very same hands which crafted the beauty of this world.

As I connected with God in this moment, I also connected to the land, realizing I am but another piece on it's beautiful canvas. Nothing is strange, nothing is too different nor invasive. The land and everything that grows and roams around on it is sourced by the very same artist. It's such an incredible feeling to come to this understanding and truly embrace it. To me it's part of what I would consider "becoming one with nature."

Gaining my composure, and feeling one with the Force (or nature), I continued on my 275 mile drive to Petrified Forest National Park. I rolled into the visitor center, like pulling up to the Rebel base. First order of business–securing a wilderness permit.

National Park Girl Steals My Heart

"Do you have any experience in the backcountry?" asked the ranger.

"Yes," I replied, even though I'd only once stayed overnight in backcountry.

"Do you have the proper gear?"

"Yes." I was pretty sure I was prepared. I'd gone camping at campgrounds countless times, and I was well read on venturing into the backcountry.

"Well then, she'll take care of you." The ranger pointed to the young lady working the register in the visitor center gift shop. She was beautiful. She had a contagious smile and was naturally friendly, asking me where I was from and where I was going. She shared with me how it was her dream to visit Acadia National Park in Maine. She turned over the back of one of the calendars being sold and pointed to Bass Harbor Lighthouse. "Isn't that just beauti-

ful?" she said. I shared with her that I would be going to
Acadia in July. "I'm jealous," she said in a playful way.

She proceeded to take out a large white binder that
had been hidden behind the desk. It was full of wilderness
information and forms for backcountry permits. She
showed me a map of the wilderness area which was separated into five zones. She made a recommendation on where
to go and told me it would be great to visit the Onyx Bridge
– a nearly complete tree, fallen and petrified, forming a
bridge over a wash. The paper she gave me had a picture of
the bridge on it and the GPS coordinates.

I filled out the paperwork and she gave me instructions. I was to take the wilderness permit with me at all
times and return it to the visitor center when I return the
following morning. If I were to return before the Visitor
Center opened I could hang my permit on the door. The
piece of paper had a sort of wire string so that it could hang,
most intentionally to hang from, a backpack. She told me to
park at the Painted Desert Inn, and from there descend a
steep trail into the canyon wilderness area. There would be
no trails nor markings, and I would be free to camp anywhere at least one mile into the wilderness area. I also had
to set up camp before 8:00 p.m.

This moment was exciting. Just the thought of having an official wilderness permit from the National Park service was super cool. It made me feel like big stuff. I knew I
wouldn't be able to keep the permit forever so I took a picture to document the momentous occasion. I then, of
course, bought a pin and left.

I sat out in my car thinking about the young lady who issued me the permit. She intrigued me. She did not fit the stereotype of someone I would expect to find working for the National Park Service. My limited experience and ignorance sort of led me to this idea that most young ladies who work for the National Park Service are tall, blond, thin, athletic, and rather stern. There's nothing wrong about that. It's attractive in its own way, but this young lady seemed more like a city girl who one day fell in love with nature and never turned back. She was short, African American, and had a personality that ran free. I felt like in our interaction there was something– chemistry, an instant connection. I had to do something about this.

Typically I am very passive in my interactions with people. This approach probably naturally formed out of low self-esteem in my younger years. The thought passing through the back of my mind is: *If someone cares about me enough to talk to me, let them instigate the conversation, otherwise keep to myself.* It's certainly not the best approach, and I had been working on becoming more bold and proactive in forming relationships. And so I thought, *What can I do?* It would be too forward to give her my number since we just met and she lived in Arizona and I in Kentucky, but there had to be some way to stay in contact. I had an idea! I just started a travel blog while utilizing the free wi-fi on the airplane. I would give her the link to my blog, and therefore she would have a way to stay connected with me. I tore a piece of paper out of my journal, wrote down the link, and went back into the visitor center.

"I just wanted to give you the link to my travel blog because I am going to upload pictures from Acadia later this summer."

It all seemed like a good idea, but unfortunately the summer came and went, and I never added a single thing to that blog. I left the solitary entry about Death Valley remain. Now I don't even remember how to access it. So this fanciful connection with this National Park gal is gone, but I'll always remember her. She was very unique.

The previous summer when I was in Zion National Park I remember sitting somewhere at the trailhead to the Narrows after completing my journey. There were two guys, probably college age, sitting nearby.

"There are so many hot girls on the trail," one said. The other confirmed it.

"I need to have like a card or something with my number on it to pass out."

I'll never forget this because it truly and comically resonated with me. There's something really attractive about a woman who embraces nature and adventure. Part of it is simply the thought of having not only a companion but a companion to adventure with. Physically, a lot of the young ladies out on the trails are very fit, and fitness is such an attractive thing as it displays health, vitality, and says something about self-worth. Also anyone seriously adventuring into the parks has to have a certain level of intellect-because intellect is needed to brave the wild. Although nature can be a place of peace it requires alertness, planning, and constant decision making. Lastly, most people who venture into the wild know themselves because they must know their limits and know how far they can stretch those limits. There is something very attractive about people who really are in tune with themselves and know who they are.

Maybe one day I will have an adventure babe, but for now I venture alone. And here I was with my wilderness pass in hand, on the brink of a new adventure, and ready to explore the Petrified Forest.

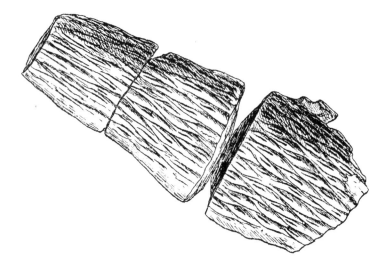

The Petrified Forest and the Wildness Within

The term "wilderness" to me typically evoked images of dense forest growth, tall conifers, meandering rivers, and abundance of wildlife. I had not associated wilderness with mounds of petrified wood chips, a dried up wash, and a maze of peculiar rock formations looking as if they had been painted every shade of orange and pink. This was my experience in the Wilderness Area of the Petrified Forest National Park, and although it was not what I had expected it topped my list of favorite experiences in nature.

My first order of business when I arrived at the park was securing a wilderness permit. Once I was able to do that I had nearly a full day ahead of me to see the sites of the park before descending into the Wilderness Area. With my Star Wars soundtrack playing, to accompany the otherworld environment, I drove from one site to another taking in the traditional tourist features of the park.

First I walked the Giant Logs Interpretive Trail behind the Rainbow Forest Visitor Center. A small pathway
meandered around many large pieces of petrified wood in
the lashing wind. The main feature was the largest piece of
intact petrified trunk called "Old Faithful" named by Jane
Mather, wife of the National Park Service's first director Stephen Mather. She thought this piece of petrified wood was
to the Petrified Forest National Park as the Old Faithful
geyser was to Yellowstone. I had not yet been to Yellowstone but I thought, *surely it's Old Faithful surpasses this one in
beauty and grandeur.* I discovered throughout my exploring of
the park that there are many things far more intriguing than
this piece of petrified wood.

Petrified wood in and of itself is interesting though,
and the park has a fascinating history. Through the visitor

"Old Faithful"

center information and interpretive trails I learned that it is
believed that Arizona and Panama used to be connected and
were a dense jungle. Then a enormous sudden flood separated the land mass and took out the entire forest. The trees
were buried under mineral rich sediment and volcanic ash
where they were protected and crystallized. As the rock and
land eroded over time the petrified wood became exposed.
I found two things very fascinating about this. First, I've
been to the jungles of Panama, and it's astounding to think
that this land was once shared with Panama. The picto-
graphs even showed dinosaurs roaming the landscape- how
cool. Secondly, this massive and immediate flood is totally
accounted for in the book of Genesis in the Bible. It's what
we refer to as Noah's flood. This was the first time I'd heard
of a giant flood in a National Park, but throughout the
course of the trip I would encounter in park after park a
massive flood being presented as the cause and formation of
many things.

My exploration of the park took me across from the
visitor center to Long Logs loop- a very "Star Wars-esque"
trail. It's true that I ran part of the trail, pretending I was
wielding a lightsaber and being chased by an inquisitor, and
I did try and imagine an Imperial ship descending upon me.
No one else was out there so I could indulge in my imagination.

Connected to the Long Logs Loop was a short trail
leading to the Agate House– a log cabin made of petrified
wood. The natives that lived in this land would build shelters out of the petrified forest wood. The National Park Ser-

Agate House

vice reconstructed one of such shelters. Here I dropped the Star Wars pretending and imagined what it would be like long ago to call this place home, gazing out the window of my petrified house into the endless expanse of wispy grass and petrified wood with a sky so large and expansive. It was a quiet and desolate world. I love how the National Parks are not only rich in beauty but also in history. When I read something in the parks about how the inhabitants once lived, I like to do more than simply collect that knowledge. I like to imagine and picture that existence for myself.

Back in my car I drove deeper into the park and stopped to hike the short Blue Mesa loop. Here rock formations were the main attraction. They appeared as giant colorful mounds composed of grey, blue, purple, and green mudstone. The path descended and slithered around these rock formations making the tourist seem very puny in relation.

From here I proceeded to the remains of old Route 66 where an abandoned vehicle pays tribute to the once roadway. I then stopped at Pintado Point overlook where I could look down into the canyon of the wilderness area. Here the colors were rich red and pink. Apart from the wilderness area I was looking into, most of the park was on largely flat and level ground and the wind was remarkably strong and ever present. Apart from the dark color of the petrified wood, both the grass and the rock formations, although full of color, were all sort of pale. This dull pale sort of filter covers my memory. But here, looking into the wilderness area, things were different. A diverse landscape of warm color invited me in. It was time!

I drove to the Painted Desert Inn which is no longer in service but is an adobe style building preserved as a national landmark. Here I would leave my car and descend in-

to the wilderness. In the parking lot I had dinner which consisted of beef jerky, almonds, an apple, and a Cliff bar. I then packed my backpack for the backcountry. I document exactly what I packed– Grand Trunk pillow, lightweight sleeping bag, Kelty, 2 flashlights, camera, phone, e-trek 10 gps, long underwear, contacts, glasses, miniature toothbrush, 3 liters of water, electrolyte gummies, and a Cliff Bar. There was a nice bathroom accessible from the outside at the Painted Desert Inn. I took advantage of it and made sure I brushed my teeth really well since I wouldn't have quite the opportunity in the wild.

I then began my descent from the plateau on foot on

Painted Desert Inn

a small steep path that rounded some switchbacks and then dumped me into the canyon to explore. I felt so small and so free. I was truly ecstatic. The beauty of it all was astounding, the freedom–incredible, and the possibilities for exploration–inspiring. I had never felt so free in my life. The girl who issued me the permit told me there was only one other permit she had issued that day, so I knew I was largely alone, that this whole endless canyon was my own world to explore. I had plugged into my etrek GPS the coordinates for the Onyx Bridge, where it was suggested I camp. As I was following my GPS the route took me past the camp of the beholders of the one other wilderness pass. They had found an astounding place to set up camp. The sun was setting between two rock formations and their tent was situated perfectly in front of the majestic scene.

"Oh, guys. It looks like we have another hiker." I was spotted. The soccer-mom-type-of-a-gal jubilantly approached me. She reached out to shake my hand. "What's your name?"

"I'm Josh."

"Josh is here, kids!" she turned back to announce to her family. This was very peculiar. I knew her kids had no clue who I was. They were unfazed.

"You found a great place to set up camp," I said, even though I looked down at my GPS and they were not a mile from the entrance. They were not following the proximity rules. I am a stickler for rules.

"You are welcome to camp with us," she invited.

"Thanks, but I'm actually looking for this bridge. I

pulled out the paper my crush in the visitor center had given me. It showed a small picture of the petrified wood bridge.

"Josh is going to a bridge, kids!" she exclaimed back to her family.

I didn't understand her referencing me by name to her kids who hadn't even met me. It was very odd. I also found it peculiar she would invite me to camp with her family without knowing anything about me except for my name.

"You want to camp with us?" She invited me again.

"No thanks. I'm going to find this bridge," I politely responded.

"Can I take a picture of you?" I am not accustomed to strangers wanting to take my picture, but I didn't see there being any problem with this. So she took two pictures

of me with her smartphone and thanked me. I was on my way. I was baffled and I still am to this day. She seemed sober and with it yet her actions were so strange, and I wonder why she wanted a picture of me.

I also wonder what her husband was thinking. I assume that's who the man setting up camp with the kids was. He said nothing and was just as unfazed as the children. If I had a wife and she was taking pictures of a stranger and inviting him to camp with us I might have a bit of a problem with that.

However, I carried on. Most of my hike was at an even lower level as I trekked through the ravine of a wide wash. I had heard on the radio in the morning, while approaching the park, there was a zero percent chance of rain, so I figured I'd be safe in the wash. At times the wash was as deep as my height, other times a little bit taller or shorter. It felt like I was on some large avenue leading to somewhere but really I was headed nowhere, not even the Onyx Bridge, because I couldn't find it. The sun was setting and my GPS was sending me around in circles. It was clear that the Onyx Bridge was simply not there. Perhaps it had been washed away or buried when water did flow through this area.

At 8:00p.m. I set up Kelty within the wash on a sand bar jutting off at one side. The sand was very soft like that of a beach, and I knew this would be a great place to camp since I would not have much to sleep on except the bottom of my tent and a thin sleeping bag.

I set my tent up to face a very large rock formation, almost appearing as a mountain by which the moon appeared. It was stunningly beautiful, but as much as I tried to photograph it, I simply could not capture the scene. The desert air was cooling off very quickly, so I changed into my long underwear. I ate my electrolyte gummies, drank some water, and gave into complete relaxation. I opened my tent door flap, rested my head against my pillow in my tent, buried my feet in the sand just outside my tent, and took in the incredible view before me. I felt at peace and had no concerns. Everything I needed was with me and

nothing extra. It was a special moment– one of those extremely rare moments that you know are gifts. I soaked up the beauty of the starry sky, breathed the cool night desert air, and drifted to sleep.

I slept very well next to the bright glow of the

moon, and I woke up with the warm sun. It was an incredible feeling to wake up in a world of my own, where I was free to go anywhere. Although the possibilities were endless I felt determined in the morning to find the Onyx Bridge. After an hour of searching I still had no luck. I did however have a great and rather thrilling time climbing to the top of a giant mound sticking up in the desert. The views from atop were amazing. I could see for miles around in all directions. The bad part was, I had not taken into account how I would come down from this thing. I searched all perimeters of this island. No route looked easy. Every possible route looked like it would involve a falling component. It was rather scary, but I chose a route. I slid down on sharp jagged pieces of petrified wood, surfing my way down the crystals. My heart was rapidly beating in exhilaration and fear. This would be the first of many times in this adventure I would climb up somewhere high not knowing how to get down. This time I descended unscathed. I wouldn't be so lucky next time.

Another mistake I made was that I had not marked a waypoint of where I began my descent from the Painted Desert Inn into the canyon the day before. I had to rely on pure instinct to guide me back. I did though; not a problem. After a few miles of hiking I could see the Painted Desert Inn way up on the edge of of the canyon rim. It was a relief.

Back on the high ground of the park I turned in my wilderness permit at the Painted Desert Visitor Center, said goodbye to the lovely Jaquacia who had issued me the permit, and considered how, although brief, this had been perhaps my favorite experience in nature thus far. The Wilderness Area of the Petrified Forest National Park definitely rests towards the top of my list.

In my car I programed my GPS to take me to the next leg of my adventure into the Navajo Nation.

The Wonder of Horseshoe Bend

The sun quietly rested for a moment on the desert horizon, sending a warm glow across the red rock expanse. It was careful and gracious enough to leave space for a cooler nighttime air to soothe the sun scorched land and let my lungs breathe deeply and at ease.

Time froze as I peered over into the most miraculous sculpture– a carving deep into the land, rounded to a perfect horseshoe, capturing light in the most intricate and intimate ways, housing the famous Colorado River. Something like this just doesn't happen. It is crafted, for it is beautiful, engaging, capturing the spectator in awe. Canyons like this dig into the soul, carving into you the realization that there is beauty that exists beyond what you can imagine, beyond the surface, and this is only a sliver of it. It takes you by surprise and you are stunned.

I think rivers, canyons, mountains, prairies, everything we find in nature is rich in meaning and designed to draw us back to the creator if we stop and listen. Mountains help us put our lives in perspective. Canyons show us there is so much more below the surface of life. Sometimes these things are just a testament to the beauty and wonder of God.

As I was awestruck by Horseshoe Bend I also was energized to find the perfect view spot to capture what I could in pictures. There were many people around, some laying on the ground with their eyes looking over the canyon

rim and some seated and poised so majestically with the canyon and sunset before them. Many photographers congregated with their tripods at just the right angle, and mothers scolded their children for getting to close to the edge. And there was me, alone at peace, yet jumping and fluttering inside, excited to take in such an iconic view.

I suppose it all sort of overtook me in three phases: the peaceful awe, the restless excitement, and the deep inspiration.

I looked down at the low-lying peninsula in the canyon with the Colorado rushing around it. What a peculiar place, trapped inside a canyon yet surrounded by immense beauty and a mighty river. What would it be like to be down there, perhaps live down there at where the lands meets the very turning point of the river, to wake up and fall asleep to the rush of the river? These thoughts in this very moment inspired me to the creation of a character who now plays a large role in a novel I am writing. He lives in such a place. At this point the novel was a year in the making at about fifty pages. The entire novel is inspired by my experiences in nature.

As I left Horseshoe Bend after a brief stay, I certainly was assured that it was worth the stop. Although technically a part of the Glen Canyon National Recreation Area it is not tucked away in a park. Right off the highway there is a large dirt parking lot and a .63 mile hike up a hill and down to the canyon rim.

When I left Horseshoe Bend it was time to restock on food and supplies in Page, Arizona. I was to meet a friend of mine, Dom, at Jacob Lake Campground in Kaibab National Forest, and we were planning to have dinner over a fire. I also needed to think ahead and get food and water for our stay at Bryce Canyon National Park, which would commence the following day. So good ol' loyal Wal-Mart once again provided what I needed. Here I also bought a heavier green sleeping bag, having learned it gets cold in the desert at these high altitudes. At the store I noticed quite a few people I had seen at Horseshoe Bend. They were also restocking for their own adventures. The spirit of natural recreation was in the air.

Fifteen miles removed from Wal-Mart, on my way to Jacob Lake, I discovered that I was running out of gas. I was in the middle of nowhere, so regretfully I had to turn around and drive back into Page for gas to avoid getting stranded.

As I was approaching Jacob Lake Campground I was no longer in desert but in a ponderosa pine forest. I had passed around a dozen deer hanging out along the side of the road. I had been in contact with Dom about the campsite. He had arrived before me. When I got there I was excited to see a familiar face that I hadn't seen for a few years, but I was also quick to get down to business and set up my tent in the dark. I broke out True Blue, because it was cold and I wanted my better insulated tent. I also blew up my air mattress (which I do by the power of my own lungs) because I wanted to get a good night's sleep.

I built a fire, cooked chicken sausages, and talked with Dom about our adventures thus far. I shared with him my amazement with the Petrified Forest and journey across the Navajo Nation. As we were talking we heard strange animal yelping sounds in the distance. We speculated if they were coyotes or turkeys– but I don't think either. It was a group of some wild animals making the most unusual noise. With the strange sounds in the background we coordinated a plan for the following day and then went to sleep.

It had been a long and full day. I had begun the day waking up in the Wilderness Area of the Petrified Forest. I hiked back to my car and drove all the way through the Navajo Nation, visiting the Hubell Trading Post National Historic Site, Canyon de Chelly National Monument, Monument Valley Navajo National Park, and Horseshoe Bend. Tomorrow Dom and I would venture into the wonders of Bryce Canyon National Park where altitude and desert heat would get to me.

ONWARD TO BRYCE CANYON

"So, where is the lake?" the camper questioned.

"It dried up three million years ago," the campground host replied.

I lay in my tent laughing to myself. This is what I woke up to this morning. I knew Jacob Lake was just the name of the campground and no lake existed. I think this other camper was a bit surprised though. If he was planning a vacation on the lake I'm sure he was disappointed.

Once again I quickly began packing up camp. The goal was to make it to Bryce Canyon National Park and secure a campsite since nothing could be reserved. I wanted a spot specifically at the North Campground. I had a backup plan if the campground was full and that was to camp at King Creek in the Dixie National Forest. But while packing up camp early at Jacob Lake I was determined to get there and find a site. One of the many great things about this area of the West is that the sun rises so early, between four and five this time of the year, so it's easy to get an early start.

Dom was not at camp when I awoke, but this was expected. He planned to take an early excursion to the North Rim of the Grand Canyon forty-four miles away. I opted out of this, because I was tired and wanted to sleep just a bit longer. I had already seen the Grand Canyon, although only the South Rim. Numerous people I encounter brag about the North Rim, but after trekking through the wilderness of the Petrified Forest and navigating all the way across the Navajo Nation I was exhausted and didn't want to get up any earlier than what I had already planned. When Dom returned to camp, he told me he spotted and took pictures of bison along the way. His bison photos, just like all his photos, were amazing.

Leaving Jacob Lake, Dom followed me in his mom's SUV that he had borrowed for the summer. The drive was

Bison Photo by Dom

beautiful, through green and mountainous regions of Utah. We stopped at a Family Dollar in Kanab. I had been here the year before en route to Coral Pink Sand Dunes State Park, and I knew this was a last stop opportunity for food and supplies for a long distance. I told Dom to get what he wanted because this was it. I found it odd that he chose to buy rice and a tin container and utensil to cook it over the fire. However, I bought pizza pockets because I figured I could cook them over the fire on marshmallow sticks, so who am I to judge? I also bought some Gatorade. I first discovered lime and cucumber Gatorade here the previous year, before it was available anywhere in middle America.

With our odd food choices packed away in our vehicles we proceeded to Bryce Canyon. Approaching the park there were a number of hotels, obviously catering to park visitors, but it was not excessive nor tacky, and the road was still wide open. Bryce Canyon National Park has a gated entrance like a number of the National Parks in the West. At the entrance booth I showed my NPS pass and ID in exchange for a park map and newspaper. I asked the employee if he thought I could find a campsite. He checked the time. "Oh, nine o'clock. I think you'll find one."

By this point I had lost Dom somewhere on the road, but I didn't mind. We talked about this. I'd find a campsite and call him, if cell service was available, if not I'd meet him in the visitor center. The North Campground was close to the park entrance, and when I got there it was filling up fast. I had to drive deep into the campground and up a hill. I settled for the second site I found open. It just so happened to be perfect. It was right next to the slope of a hill which rolled down into pine forest, and there was enough space for both of us to pitch a tent. I felt relieved.

Trying to get a hold of Dom was tricky because cell service was spotty, but we managed to communicate. He found me and we both set up our tents. Then we went down to place the camping fee in an envelope at the collection post and proceed to the visitor center, as it is customary for me to watch the park films before exploring the parks. I learned how the landscape within Bryce Canyon changes every winter season as the snow and ice causes hoodoos to fall. Apart from the theater the visitor center was very busy. The line to talk to an employee at the desk to inquire about hikes and plans was very long, stretching through the expanse of the whole center to the front door.

After our brief stop in the visitor center we prematurely embarked on one of my most challenging hikes ever. The high elevation combined with running out of water and forgetting sunscreen made for some difficult times, and falling off the trail down a rock slide into the canyon onto a cactus just added to the challenges. One can rightfully say I was grossly unprepared this time.

Falling Into Bryce Canyon

"Don't do it. You're going to end up as one of those people we read about in the book."

I had just finished telling Dom about a book called *Death, Daring, and Disaster: Search and Rescue in the National Parks*, and now I was about to do something a bit daring myself.

I had hiked across a very narrow rock promontory, standing above Bryce Canyon. It couldn't have been more than three feet wide. I wanted a picture from atop. At one point there was a giant step. I had to place my arms on the higher ground and push the rest of my body up. While I was successful at reaching the plateau, my trekking pole scraped against the ground and came loose from my backpack. Gravity snatched it from me. I saw it plummeting and somersaulting down the canyon, bouncing off the rocks and echoing around me.

"I'm going to go get it!" is what I proclaimed, and that is when Dom pointed out the absurdity of the idea. I was telling him about the book I had been reading and all the stupid and ridiculous things people do in National Parks which put them in danger. He was clearly listening well to me, because his pointing out of the parallel between the present situation and the book was well stated. He made an appealing case to not pursue my run away trekking pole, but regardless, I didn't listen to him.

This trekking pole and me have been on way too many adventures together for it to end like this. My cousin Jonathan bought it for me when we both went to Yosemite National Park for the first time. This was my first major hiking and camping trip, and it was an amazing life experience. This trekking pole was with me the whole time. Also, the pole could adjust easily to varying heights. I could jab it into the ground and unscrew its handle to fasten on my camera and have a sturdy monopod. It was so practical, so useful. It was a gift. I didn't know how much something like this cost. I'm frugal. I was going to go retrieve it.

…Or at least I was going to thoroughly assess the situation. So the canyon wasn't very deep at this point. It was probably thirty feet down. It wasn't a straight drop. There was a very steep diagonal slope of crumbled rock. I assessed the possibility that I could sort of surf my way down the crumbling rock. I turned around to Dom. "Make sure the camera is recording," I instructed. This had to be properly documented.

Recounting this experience I'm not sure if the next

event was a part of the plan or if gravity took me by surprise, but next thing I know I'm sliding down into the canyon, uncontrollably. I couldn't stay standing. I'm falling. My feet are pushing and digging into crumbles of red rock before me but it's not enough to break the fall. The rocks are crudely climbing up into my pants. I look down and I don't know how this is going to end. *Dom is right. I'm going to end up in that book*, I'm thinking to myself. Then in all the excitement and distress it comes to a screeching halt with my rear planted on a cactus.

Ouch!

I stood up. Thankfully this cactus was wimpy so no real damage was done to my posterior, but very fine cactus needles were clinging to the back of my gym shorts and it was not comfortable. I grabbed my trekking pole and we were reunited. Mission accomplished. Now, to get back up! It looked daunting. This was not going to be easy if possible at all. I scouted the perimeter of the promontory rock formation I fell from. The only chance of getting back up would be from the way I came down. With that thought in mind panic set in. I could be stuck down here. I didn't even know this place. I only got here a few hours ago. I did know that mountain lions live here. *I'm going to be stuck in a canyon all night with mountain lions!* Perilous thoughts started to snowball out of control. *Okay, I've got to get out of here,* I told myself.

I began my ascent. It was so steep that I realized once I began, there was no backing down. There was no grip to successfully back down. It would entail another fall, and perhaps not as merciful as the initial fall. Gripping onto the crumbling rock was of course useless, and I started to slide backwards, so I grabbed onto part of the canyon wall jutting out. This had to be my route up. I found cracks and rock shelves to place my feet on, and when possible I balanced one foot on the crumbling rock and the other on the canyon wall. At this point my heart was racing, feeling as if it was going to jump right out of my chest and take off on a marathon. I realized this was not safe but there was no other way upward. In this moment I remembered bouldering with my brother at a climbing gym the month before in Louisville, Kentucky. It was only my second time bouldering and I didn't do so bad. This canyon wall in Bryce Canyon required the same skills, the same focus and determination. I stretched my arms and legs to their widest extent, said a quick prayer, and started pulling myself up, unsure if my efforts would prove fruitful, but it worked! I eventually made it to the plateau.

I was so thankful and excited to be safe and on a trail, and ready to make a commitment to never do anything so careless like that again.

I raced back over to Dom, who had taken a seat to relax during my daring shenanigan.

"What an experience!" I exclaimed.

"Was it worth it?" he nonchalantly questioned.

Definitely worth it if you captured it all on video, I thought to myself. Come to find out, none of it was recorded except that last piece of dialogue. With disappointment, but a rivet-

ing adventure tale now in my pocket and a sturdy loyal trekking pole, we continued on our journey around the Fairyland Loop.

My Journey on the Fairland Loop

"I just can't go on any longer," I told myself. This was definitely not the positive self talk I needed to get myself through this hike. This trail seemed longer, hotter, and more draining than I had imagined. I mean after all, how treacherous can a trail named "Fairyland Loop" be? It sounds so dainty.

It was a ten miles hike. I knew this, but somehow in the excitement of being here in Bryce Canyon National Park and meeting up with my friend Dom, I had forgotten two essential things, sunscreen and a sufficient amount of water. On top of this I had already fallen into the canyon onto a cactus. This trail experience was a little rough, but it was also amazing, and I'd do it all again if given the opportunity.

The name Fairyland Loop is quite appropriate for such a trail because it's such a fanciful, other worldly, colorful trail, with bizarre rock formations and hoodoos around every winding turn.

Hoodoos are columns of rocks that are soft, (if we can consider rocks soft for a moment), but these formations have a hard capstone protecting the towers of rocks from complete erosion. They stick up like pillars and are a rather rare geological feature. I have seem them in Arizona and Kentucky but not to the extent to which they are present in Bryce Canyon. This park is known for them and they are everywhere. The Fairyland Loop wanders around the base of many hoodoos and descends to the base of the canyon. The descent has one walking by sections of bright white sand and soft orange rocks. It meanders around the canyon floor, through sparse pine forest, and at one point passes by Window Arch, an iconic feature of the park- a window of erosion through a large rock protrusion which

Window Arch

looks like a fanciful piece of planned architecture.

As we hiked along the canyon floor Dom and I talked a lot about teaching. We are both public school teachers, but in different states, myself in Kentucky and him in Indiana. We were talking about things most people find thrilling, such as state requirements for certification, teacher evaluation methods, and professional development in our districts.

Bryce Canyon, and particularly this trail, is a very charming place. It evokes such a unique feeling from any other National Park. Inside the canyon, after getting over the possibility of encountering a mountain lion, I felt sheltered and protected as if this was a place I belonged in. The warm colors of the rock were inviting, the pines relaxing. In many ways it was like walking through and being part of a very fine piece of artwork. It all seemed so intentional, designed to soothe the soul and fold me up in the arms of the Creator.

As kind as my description may have been, some realities set in. As we began to ascend a mesa out in the canyon the sun was beating harshly, and I realized I forgot to apply and pack sunscreen. The hot sun was stinging my skin. I had a light hoodie in my backpack. I put it on and stretched the hood over my head to protect me from the sun. It sufficed but added a layer of heat.

We then came to the top of the mesa and hiked out to a small promontory. A few pines stood to provide shade, and short shrubbery blanketed most of the ground. Here we gazed onto another iconic feature of the park— The Sinking

The Sinking Ship

Ship. In the distance before us a protrusion of land dipping into the canyon sinks backward, creating a convincing image of a sinking ship. The formation was named very appropriately and was definitely worth the hike.

At this point of the hike I was beginning to wear out and so I sat on the edge of the mesa. I explained to Dom how it would be such a great place to camp– a place of remote isolation, nice shade and beautiful views in all directions.

Unfortunately we could not camp here, we had to continue on. The trail slithered around some narrow passes down, up, and around the canyon. On this final leg of this hike I ran out of water. I had only brought with about a liter and probably needed about three liters. The National Park Service advises in arid climates to be prepared with a liter per hour.

Finally, after about 8 miles, the trail guided us back on the canyon rim where the main infrastructures of the park lie– the entrance, visitor center, lodge, roads, overlooks, and campgrounds. It was still a two mile hike back to our campground. I was extremely weary. The fact that this was my first major hike this trip at high elevation contributed to this exhaustion. I don't think my body was ready for it. It had not adjusted, and the realization of this was the moment when the thought crept in, *I just can't do this anymore.*

My hiking pace began to slow down dramatically and I was forcing my body to continue. Dom also expressed his tiredness. He was in all the same forgetful predicaments as myself, but he plowed on, leaving me literally in the rocky dust. I needed a break. I sat down on the canyon rim with my legs hanging over, resting on a slope of rock slide which fell beneath the stance of some large hoodoos. I casually pushed some rock with my feet, listening to a pleasing pinging hollow sound as the small rocks and pebbles clanked into the hoodoos. I did this a couple of times until I realized I was abusing the landscape and needed to let things be. I also wasn't sure if there were other hikers below. I didn't want to be showering them with rocks. I picked myself up and hiked the longest two miles of my life, along the rim back to camp.

This predicament of exhaustion was ironic because I had secretly passed major judgment on Dom, thinking he was ill-equipped and lacked the experience for this hike. So it was fitting and justified that he left me behind and crossed the finish line before me. My pride needed to be humbled.

Once back at camp I drowned myself in some Ga-torade and then water. We had anticipated taking showers and drove to the general store within the park where the coin showers were located. However, they had just closed up shower access for the day. The general store was in a log cabin structure and was well equipped with food and sup-plies. I enjoyed a piece of everything pizza and a Chobani yogurt. I sat the porch out front for a minute and took in the peacefulness of the evening.

Back at camp I organized my trunk. On this trip I was living out of my rental car, and most everything was organized in a specific location in the trunk. Clothes were in the far rear organized in piles. To the right was the camping section of all tents, flashlights, and other gear. To the left was the "kitchen," where extra storage bags, paper towels, and canned food items resided. Behind the clothes was my suitcase which only contained things I did not need immedi-ate access to. On top of that was the main food storage unit – a thin plastic tub filled with nuts, dried berries, and pro-tein and granola barns. On top of that was a backpack which served as electronic department, with my Chrome-book, spare batteries, cords, and cameras. I had this down to a science. Going on a camping trip and not being orga-nized doesn't work well for me, because I end up spending so much time looking for things in the car or not realizing all I have with me. Everything needs to have a place and be ready to be accessed on demand.

After I got organized I built a campfire with Dom as the sun slipped below the horizon. We sat there by the fire

with a sense of accomplishment from hiking the Fairyland
Loop and having our vehicles organized. I was ready to
make s'mores but discovered my chocolate had completely
melted to liquid. First Dom cooked his rice dish and I
cooked my pizza pockets. Then we made
our *chocolateless* s'mores as the stars began to make their
bright appearance and campers retired for the night. Tomorrow we would explore more of Bryce Canyon. (Note:
pizza pockets do not taste very good cooked over a fire.)

Recollection and Wonder

Most of my memory of Bryce Canyon is painted in warm shades of orange and dressed in a whimsical fashion with forest animals tramping around and everything being just about right. Bryce Canyon is a lasting deep breathe of fresh air that will remain vividly captured in my memory. No other park comes close to capturing its unique combination of forest, desert, and hoodoo wonderland. I will long for it's hot dry sunny days and cool refreshing star-filled nights, where the air feels hollow and easy to breath, perfectly accommodating the camping visitor.

On this second day in Bryce Canyon I began with a hike. Dom did not join because he needed to seek internet and complete homework for a class he was taking— a very unfortunate circumstance I must say. I began my hike on the Queen's Garden Trail and continued on the Navajo Loop. The trails were narrow and crowded. Many people were en-

joying the wonders of Bryce Canyon. At a few turns in the
trail I had to wait on people in front of me. The trails
wound around many hoodoos, shimmied through slot canyons, and passed under natural arches, all in manageable 2.7
mile hike.

I'm not sure if it's the names of the trails such as
"Queen's Garden" and "Fairyland Loop" that influence my
perception, but Bryce Canyon does remind me in a rounda-
bout way of Alice in Wonderland. Maybe it's in part because
of such colorful geological oddities and it's trails meandering
and twisting around in such a whimsical fashion to arrive at
a singular spot. A sense of wondrous suspense accompanied
me on these trails, for I never knew what was around each
bend and twist in the trail, what seemingly impossible geological feature would stand before me, or what colors would
so strikingly comprise the landscape.

During my morning hike I came to a bend in the trail
where a squirrel stood upright, poised on two feet, as if waiting to draw attention from the hikers. It looked different
than the typical squirrels we have in the Midwest. I later
learned that it was a golden-mantled ground squirrel. The
way it was poised looked as if it was accustomed to posing
for pictures. It wasn't the least bit concerned by my proximity. It didn't budge as I knelt down to take it's picture. It was
just the sort of adorable woodland creature one would expect to find in such a whimsical place. Squirrel pictures always run the risk of being commonplace but this turned out
to be one of my most memorable photos from this park. It
is important to note, approaching wild squirrels is not advis-

able, and if done should be done with caution. Some squirrels in the National Parks of the West can become aggressive.

I recall the prior summer when I was in Zion, another National Park not too far away, I was short on time and
was in a hurry to get to the trailhead of the famous Narrows.
There was heavy slow-moving traffic on the pathway because a group of Asian tourists were enthralled at the sight
of squirrels and were all trying to take pictures of the creatures. I was annoyed. *It's just a squirrel*, I thought. But when
you are more carefree and have the time, I now understand
the pleasure in stopping, not to smell the roses, but to admire the squirrels.

After the photo-shoot with the squirrel I continued
on my hike, passing large thin hoodoos towering above as if
enormous fins to guide the planet through the galaxy. As the
canyon narrowed to almost a slot canyon a pine tree strikingly stood grounded reaching for the sky– a location where
many travelers have taken photos.

The last leg of the hike included dozens of short
switchbacks out of the canyon. Despite being man-made
these switchbacks are one of the more iconic features of the
park. I'd seen them before from various photographers, and
they appeared in Greg MacGillivray's film, *National Parks
Adventure*. As I was ascending I captured a scene that will
stick with me forever. An elderly couple most likely in their
eighties were ascending the dozens of switchbacks. They
walked extremely slow, just shy of shuffling, slowly but determined. At the curve of a switchback the husband, reached

out his hand to help his wife ascend the steep incline. I simply watched. Their actions spoke a lot. Though moving extremely slow they didn't let their age nor weakness stop them from adventure. The husband reaching out to help his nearly crippled wife ascend and round the curve was precious, speaking of the love and dedication he had for her. I'm certain they had no awareness of my presence and observations. It goes to show that the simplest and most ordinary of your actions can have a lasting impression on others.

I wondered how many adventures this couple had gone on before. Were they seasoned park explorers, just continuing to do what they love and not letting old age stop them, or was this because they had not gotten out when they were younger, so now they decided to see what they could? I prefer to entertain the first and imagine this couple held tons of adventure stories and a wealth of experience, and nothing would stop them from having more adventures.

Back on the high ground I got in my car and decided to drive the length of the park and get a complete feel for the place. The park infrastructure was very simple with one main road that traverses the expanse of the canyon rim and numerous spots one can pull over to take in beautiful vistas of the canyon expanse. The road climbs up into brisker, more densely wooded areas and extends all the way to Yovimpa Point, which during this visit was closed due to repair.

After my self guided tour I drove back to the general store to attempt to take a shower again. It was a success. However, I forgot a towel, but it wasn't much of a problem.

The climate was so dry that I quickly dried off. There is nothing more refreshing than stepping out of the shower into a hot but dry climate. The air feels amazing and I feel totally refreshed. After my shower I then bought myself another piece of pizza and a Greek yogurt from the general store. After enjoying these on the porch I drove to the Bryce Canyon Lodge, picked up a couple postcards, and found a quiet nook near the lobby. I was surprised to find Dom there working on his homework. I told him about the trails I hiked and the beautiful drive and then sat down to write my postcards. I wrote on a panoramic postcard to my parents and then wrote to two other postcard buddies.

When both Dom and I came to completion of our tasks I convinced Dom to go on the park drive. I accompanied him, having enjoyed it so much the first time. I'm glad I did go a second time and was able to share the experience with Dom. Dom had his borrowed SUV packed with gear for a summer of adventure. His plan was similar to mine, to road trip and explore the great American West. His trip was less planned than mine. I had campsites reserved for every night, and even had Plan As and Plan Bs for parts of my trip. Dom was more carefree, willing to travel wherever the winds swept him or the roads led him. One notable thing he had in the SUV was a drone. Dom is really into photography and the latest in technology and was hoping to catch some great drone pictures along the way. Drone use however is prohibited in most National Parks, but he did tell me how he sent it in flight at Horseshoe Bend– a few days before. When it was out above the river in the canyon, it ran out of battery power and started plummeting towards the Colorado River. Moments before impact it had a spike of energy and was able to be flown back to safety.

As I was ascending the canyon rim a second time with Dom I really took in the stark contrast between the two sides of the road. One side of the road boasted the Bryce Canyon and all it's warm orange display. The other side was all thick pines, dark green, no orange, looking like the forest of the northwest.

Along the drive Dom and I got out of the SUV at numerous viewpoints but eventually decided we wanted to race the clock and get back to the main section of the park to Sunset Point before sunset. We failed. We arrived at Sunset Point just moments late. Both of us wanted to arrive there at sunset for different reasons. Dom wanted to take pictures, and I wanted to be there because I read in the park newsletter how Stephen Mather, the first director of the National Park Service, sat at this point admiring the canyon at sunset and here decided he wanted to protect this as a National Park. I wanted to put myself in his perspective and gaze upon the canyon at sunset, looking at it with the same value and admiration Mather did.

Despite having missed the sunset the view was still gorgeous, and the canyon was painted deep orange and dark purple. Opposite the canyon the sky was bright pink with the silhouettes of tall pines on display. Dom started talking to another photographer all in technological terms beyond my amateur understanding. I wandered off and lost Dom, but eventually we were reunited at the SUV and headed back to camp.

At camp I roasted some slices of ham lunch meat over the fire and cooked a can of corn at the fire's edge. Dom was hoping, all during the day, that he would get to see a Utah prairie dog, an endangered species only present in Bryce Canyon out of all the National Parks. Despite his desire he had no luck. The following morning I had success, but the creatures were easily startled and too fast to be captured by camera.

This second night was our last night of sitting around a campfire in Bryce Canyon National Park. This National Park visit was quintessential, beautiful, challenging, calming, and now I had stored up in my mind a previously unimaginable landscape to explore again in recollection and wonder.

Utah, My Love

Utah is an incredible place. Although it's a popular place for hikers, in my travels it has often seemed like I've had the whole place to myself. On my way to Capitol Reef National Park I hadn't passed another car in a long time. Civilization was becoming sparse. I was filled with excitement to go to this lesser known National Park.

I first learned about Capitol Reef from the *Rock the Park* show in which Jack Steward described it as a "gem." It was an intriguing episode, because the park was portrayed with such a unique balance of history and nature. Jack also described it as "The real Wild West." Growing up in, and always being confined to, the Northeast and Midwest the Wild West always seemed so unreachable and too legendary to bother with making my acquaintance, but here we were about to meet!

Prior to my arrival I knew some basics about Capitol

Reef. It was a supposed hideout for outlaws, including the infamous Butch Cassidy. It also included a commonly traveled pioneer wagon route and the restored Mormon ghost town of Fruita, situated in an oasis tucked down between the giant rock walls. It was named Capitol Reef after a giant rock feature on top of the Reef, which pioneers thought resembled the U.S. capitol building. I wanted to see it all for myself and was very curious what the "Reef" itself would look like for its a hundred mile outcropping of earth pointing to the sky.

The two hour drive from Bryce Canyon to Capitol Reef was very peaceful and marked by tranquility yet unbridled anticipation. I was driving down the long wavy landscape swooping down and rolling up to see new marvels at each crest. I had gotten another early start as to be able to secure a campsite in Fruita. As I was traveling down the open roads the morning sun was still waking up, slowly peering over mountainous deserts and lush fields of the remote Utah farmland. The temperature was brisk and in the lower fifties. The sun didn't seem to be in a hurry but stretched casually, illuminating the beauty around it, turning dark grey areas to vibrant oranges and greens. As I approached the park, red giants stood up all around me. They announced their existence boldly and reached dramatically into the sky– some layered with colors, others monotone. Between the road and these giants were just fields of sand and rocks mixed with typical desert shrubs. It very much reminded me of the landscape in Disney Pixar's original *Cars* movie. It felt like any minute I'd be pulling up to Radiator Springs.

The Reef itself jutted diagonally up into the sky, as an immense rock ledge. In the park film I learned it is believed to have formed by plates of land colliding, pushing one plate up into the air, creating this massive wrinkle in the earth's crust.

I was traveling alone. Dom had taken off in a different direction. He had forgotten to pack his camera battery and had found a place online in Moab, Utah that sold it. He was going to seek that out. When I rolled into the park I passed the small visitor center and headed straight to Fruita. I didn't have much pick of a site because the campground was small and many sites were taken.

The whole campground was flat and had a mix of green grass and desert dust. It was all fenced in so it did not have much of a wild feel. Roads were paved, sites plainly arranged. It was a very civilized campground yet very scenic, because it was tucked away between giant red walls situated in small and picturesque Fruita. I chose a site in the front left corner of the campground. I quickly set up camp. Knowing I would stay a few days I decided I would rest spaciously in True Blue. I then purchased some firewood from the campground host and headed back to the visitor center, as always, to watch the park film, purchase a pin and sticker, and ask a ranger for hiking recommendations, despite already having an agenda. I then hit the park road.

The first hike on the agenda was to Cassidy Arch. It was a 6.6 mile round-trip hike. The trail arrived at a place believed to be a hideout spot for the infamous criminal it's named after. To get there I drove on a extremely scenic dusty dirt road in an expansive area between enormous rock walls where my little rental car kicked up a large trail of dusty clouds. The giants walls and bold rock formations around me made me feel so small, as if my car was just a spec of dust. I had never seen anything like this. I carefully maneuvered my car around some sharp turns, paying attention to the location of my tires, making sure they didn't fall into any ruts or run over any sharply protruding rocks.

I came to a dirt parking-lot. There were maybe a dozen other vehicles which had ventured out here. I got out of my car, took off my shirt to cover myself in sunscreen, and made sure my Camelbak was at its water holding capacity. The sun now was fully awake and wasn't holding anything back. It was raw, sharp, and felt close by without any filter. I began my hike on a river wash and shortly took a turn left to start ascending, hiking between a multitude of fallen rocks and desert shrubs. I remember looking up in amazement wondering why I had not heard more about this place. It reminded me of the awe and grandeur of looking over Yosemite Valley, just in a different color. Mountains rolled around in every direction and rocks abruptly and strikingly reached up into the sky. The reds, oranges, browns, and even whites were layered, and at other times they swirled around.

I remember looking across the distance in awe and thanking God for the adventure and acknowledging his awesome creativity. The more places I visit and new landscapes I see the more I get to know God, as I observe the creative expressions He has poured himself into.

As I was ascending from the canyon along this path, which hugs and meanders around cliff edges, a group of three young teenage boys passed me…and then I passed them. This became a pattern until it started to become a bit awkward. I decided to let them establish a lead, as I knew I'd be stopping many times to take pictures.

As the trail reached higher ground much of it was on open exposed rock face, and the only way to know where I was going was to look for cairns. Some were small and inconspicuous, so my eyes were constantly scanning in all directions, and a few times I had to trace my steps backward to find the marker.

After 3.3 miles I reached Cassidy Arch. There was one family there, and separate from them a group of about ten boys and a couple of men. I quickly figured out that it was a Boy Scout group that had beat me here. How cool it would be to take a Boy Scout excursion to Capitol Reef! Anyone that lives in Utah is spoiled with exquisite landscapes. Utah is my wonderland and favorite state because of its beauty. I was able to recruit a Boy Scout leader to take my photo with Cassidy Arch behind me. I then sat down and rested there at the end of the trail on the open rock facing the arch. Here I was, having already seen Saguaro, the Navajo Nation, Horseshoe Bend, and Bryce Canyon, yet my adventure was still young. I already felt accomplished, yet there was much more to see and adventure to be had. Here in Capitol Reef, tucked away in Utah, I truly felt off the grid, away from it all, hidden, just like the outlaws. I had escaped the troubles of my world and was free. As always Utah makes me feel at home. Although some may dread the heat of the desert, Utah to me has felt comforting.

I have noticed many times hiking in Utah that my skin, after being exposed to the summer sun, takes on the same color of much of the rock. Utah is a place in which I could go camouflaged. It reminds me of the piece of scripture that says God formed man out of the dust of the earth. If God were to have formed me out of the dust of this earth, He picked up a scoop of Utah and molded me, and maybe that is why I love the Utah landscape so much– maybe coming to Utah is in some ways, coming home.

I let this sink in as I sat there facing Cassidy Arch. I felt that making acquaintance with Capitol Reef was more than a mere polite gesture. Capitol Reef had spoken. "Welcome…" it said, "…just make yourself at home." And so I did.

THE WAY OF THE PIONEER

"Oh you're from Kentucky? That's different," the hiker responded. I wasn't sure how to interpret this at first, but really I understood exactly what he meant. It happens to me all the time when I travel. "I've never met any visitors from Kentucky," a few rangers have told me before. Having lived many places I don't always claim I am from Kentucky, but when I do, it always summons an interesting response. Among the responses is often, "You don't sound like you are from Kentucky." This is true because I am not originally from Kentucky. I was born in Chicago and raised primarily in Massachusetts. However, my family roots run deep in the fertile soil of Illinois.

Despite not originating in Kentucky, I am quick to defend Kentucky within reason on many accounts, but I cannot deny, as a whole, many Kentuckians are not known for venturing out, and if they do it's usually to the same few places. On top of that, Capitol Reef is really venturing out—

the most remote National Park I had been to thus far.

Coming out of the Pioneer Register I came upon this hiker and his wife who inquired where I was from. The Pioneer Register is a slot canyon graffitied by carvings of pioneers and their dates of passage, dating back to the early 1800s. The Pioneer Register is an incredible place because of hundreds of names of people who passed through the narrow canyon. It's also fascinating to consider how they were traveling on stage coach, over rough rocky terrain in the desert heat, squeezing their way through rock walls. I'd want to reach out to them and say, *don't lose heart, you are almost to Fruita.*

Walking through the canyon I imagined the fear of flash floods must have been very real for the pioneers. There would have been no escape from flood waters down here, and flash floods truly do come unexpectedly. In Utah, where much of the ground is hard rock, water is not absorbed. Instead it moves and can travel from a stormy location to a place where the weather is blissfully fair. These pioneer would have had no warning of flash floods.

Looking up and marveling at the extensive register of names I noticed how some people chose to carve their names in beautiful cursive. Others had left their names carved into the wall by series of bullet holes. It would be painful to imagine how loud it must have been, with the sound of the gun shots echoing off the canyon walls. An aspect that makes this location all the more interesting is that it is unmarked. It's not behind a fence or protected in glass. It's just there, exposed on the canyon walls, and you can walk right up to and through the canyon, seeing the same views and experiencing a fragment of the same journey as these brave pioneers.

This was around mid day of my first day in Capitol Reef. I had just previously hiked up to Cassidy Arch, but now was down on the low lands. This couple I came upon asked me to take their picture inside a hollowed out hole in the canyon wall. I too asked for them to take my picture, but it didn't come out well. I am particular about my photos and my artistic eye is not always pleased when another attempts to capture my vision. We got to talking and these people told me they were from California. They had been to Death Valley, and the wife was wearing a Death Valley shirt. I took notice because that is my favorite National Park. Inquiring about what I do for work, we eventually got on the topic of Mexico City. "What's that neighborhood in the city, that's very beautiful with the home of Frida Kahlo?" The man asked.

"Coyoacan!" I exclaimed. The topic of Mexico City is also one of my favorites. I've spent a lot a time there as a student and also on various vacations. The husband advised that if I loved Mexico City I would love visiting Buenos Aires, Argentina. It just so happened to be one place I was already interested in visiting.

Upon bidding farewell to the couple, I returned to my car and the adventurous dirt road back to Fruita. I had completed my hiking agenda for the day, was tired and just wanted to rest in my little desert oasis. I had new appreciation for Fruita, having been to the Pioneer Regis-

ter and trying to put myself in the perspective of the travelers. Fruita would have been, in some ways, a paradise, with
trees providing shade, the Fremont River flowing nearby,
orchards of fruit, and villagers to accommodate. Despite the
excitement Fruita may have been to pioneers, at my
campsite, I found myself bored, which is a very rare occurrence for myself. It was too late and I was too tired to begin
another hike.

      I had studied the park map, read the newsletter, and
didn't know what else to do. I recollected my experience in
Saguaro and wrote a brief poem. After lying restless in my
tent, craving some relief from the valley heat, not knowing
what to do with myself, I realized what was missing in my
life– a book. I needed a book. I wanted to read. Reading is
relaxing, distracts from the discomforts, in this case heat
around me, and puts me in a place of peace. But I had nothing left to read, except I recalled I had my novel in the
works saved on my Chromebook. I fired up the machine
and started reading my own work. At this point I had twenty
-five pages written of the novel.

      Despite its comfort, reading didn't last long as hun-
ger was nudging me to start the fire and eat some food. I got
out of my tent, started a fire and heated a can of chicken
noodle soup. In the heat of the valley soup was not the most
enjoyable of meals, and all my water supply had turned hot,
from the day's sun. Also, during my meal, flies started to
pester me to the point of irritability with the annoying buzz
and humming around my ears, the occasional attempts to
dart at my eyes. These little flies were not my friends. I did-

n't want to spend all evening in my tent, so I figured if I climbed up to a higher elevation I might escape them. They seemed to thrive among the greenery and water of the Fruita valley. So I filled up a hydration pack, threw on a long sleeve shirt- anticipating the weather to cool down soon, walked across the road to a trailhead and took a very short hike halfway up a trail leading to the plateau above. I was very tired, my legs feeling weighted. I sat down, rested, and looked down into Fruita at the campground and an old barn next to a small field for horses. It was scenic and pictur-esque, but despite my attempt to escape, the flies followed me. Heat wasn't so much the problem, but the dryness, thirst for cold water, mixed with the pestering flies made me into a highly irritable creature. I realized the remedy I really needed was a good night's sleep. I hadn't caught up on any of the time lost after skipping over two time zones. I hiked down to my tent, brushed and flossed my teeth in the campground bathroom (because dental hygiene is never compromised when I camp) and checked into my tent for the night. I read over the poem I wrote about Saguaro, as well as a few from previous summers, and I fell asleep.

Coming Back to Life

It was only supposed to be a two mile hike but it felt like twelve. It was day two in Capitol Reef National Park, and I had set foot in the morning on the Rim Overlook Trail to catch a view of Fruita from above. Never before had I been on a trail that was so short yet seemed so long. I believe this perception was gained in part from the tedious task of maneuvering my feet around rocks, watching out for rattlesnakes, and searching for cairns to keep me en route. On top of that, add extreme heat and sun exposure. There was also the repeatedly false perception that the trail was coming to an end. I would see an outcropping of land along the rim, and assume it was the end only to find out the trail wound around and kept going. This happened maybe a half dozen times.

The trail eventually ended at Fruita Point where I looked down into the canyon. It wasn't the viewpoint that was the highlight of the trek, as it was forgettable, but what stays with me most vividly in my memory is the hike there, through shambles of broken rocks, across expansive sun baked rock faces, and through indentations and coves of sand. At one point I rested, stretching myself out in some soft sand as if reclining at the beach, but I was really in a sunken cove hidden by desert brush. At another point I sat in a smooth rock cavity, just my size, to find shelter from the sun. Although seemingly long, the trail was fun, interesting, and throughout the whole trek I was accompanied by small lizards who would blend in so fine with the landscape but suddenly scurry upon approach, causing me to flinch at their surprise.

When I was back down in Fruita, after my hike, I was very hungry and felt I had burned enough calories to earn a fruit pie sold at the little gift shop in Fruita. The town has a history of fruit harvesting and pie and jam making. I figured that in order to have the full Fruita experience I needed to have some pie. I bought an individual blackberry pie and a small cup of ice cream (the kind with a wooden stick), and I enjoyed it on a picnic table out front. This area of Fruita was quite busy now, meaning there were a few families on the premise, but it was obvious from overhearing their talking that they were just day visitors. I was able to tune out all the noise around me and write in my notebook about my experiences in the Petrified Forest.

After eating my pie I went for a walk around Fruia. I walked past the old school house, down by the river, and to a large section made into what sort of looked like a city park, with a mowed lawn and picnic tables. There I observed some very old girthy cottonwood trees. There was a placard explaining their significance, showing photos from back in the pioneer days of the same trees. Leaving this lawn area I walked by the orchard. I had read online you could pick fruit from the orchard, but it didn't look like they were allowing it at this time.

As I was walking by the orchard some mule deer walked right up to me. I was not used to deer approaching me. Deer to me have been some of the most easily frightened animals, but these deer were approaching me! I had to curve my direction so they wouldn't walk into me. I am used to deer in the Midwest and South where they are so frequently hunted. Perhaps, because of this, they have developed knowledge and instinct to avoid humans. But here, tucked away in a desert oasis, protected by the National Park Service, humans are not feared. Wherever humans go

they usually bring food, and in this area food was not in plenty, so perhaps the deers welcomed humans in hopes that humans would provide for them. I've observed in my travels that desert environments bring out boldness and aggressiveness in all creatures.

I myself was ready to aggressively search out food and water. I was craving with great intensity cold water. I was prepared with water, but my water was hot. I wanted cold water, and I craved food other than nuts, berries, and jerky I had packed away in my car. I searched in my GPS for restaurants. The nearest was a Subway, thirty miles away. Typically, by no means would I drive thirty miles just to go to a Subway, and furthermore it had been my tradition that once in a National Park for a stay not to leave it. However, the thirst and hunger was so present and nagging, that I decided that even for just a sip of cold water, thirty miles there and back would be worth it.

The miles went by quickly, and I found the Subway located inside a gas station. That Subway sandwich and water mixed with artificial lemonade syrup made me the most appreciative of beings. In the gas station I also bought a bag of Muddy Buddy Chex Mix. The sweet powdery crunch was so satisfying and so memorable, that it created a powerful association in my mind, so much so that from that point on Muddy Buddy Chex Mix has become my preferred snack on summer camping road trips.

On my way back into Fruita I stopped at the entrance sign to Capitol Reef National Park to take a picture and then I pulled over at Sunset Point. I thought the sun was soon setting, and here I could take it in. I came to discover that the sun had already set behind the reef. Nevertheless Sunset Point proved to be a beautiful viewpoint. From here I looked down into deeper canyons and up at mountains in the far distance with the giant walls of Capitol Reef to my left. I thought this place was beautiful, and it was one of those moments in which I really became aware of not only my existence but my own presence in this place. I closed my eyes for a moment to attune my ears to the quietness around me. I opened them to rediscover myself in this amazing and strikingly different landscape. I recollected where I came from, all the hardships of life I have endured, and here and now I had the will and aptitude to bring myself to remote Utah and immerse myself in its natural beauty. With all the peace surrounding me, and the spark of adventure now ablaze, I realized I was still on the front end of a large summer adventure. But already I was feeling restored, alive and free. Nature always has a way of bringing me back to life...the Subway sandwich also helped.

Trouble at Arches National Park

My heart was racing. *What do I do now?* I looked down. This
was the third time on my adventure I found myself in the
dilemma of being in a high-up location, looking below me
uneasily, wondering how to get back down. The big difference was this time there was an audience of spectators
watching me. I had to make a decision quickly. I did not
want anyone coming to my rescue. This was embarrassing.
I found myself crouched down low, legs extended, and fin-
ger-tips trying to clench the rough steep sand paper terrain.

I was at the base of Delicate Arch- the most iconic
geological feature of Utah. It wasn't enough for me to see it
and get my picture taken by it. I wanted to explore around
it. As I went to hug the arch legs and shimmy my way
around its base I lost footing, gravity cleverly pulled me. I
couldn't stay standing any longer, and as my body and
limbs were spread out across the terrain like a spider, I was

afraid that any slight movement might send me tumbling into the desert bowl below me. The bowl just below the arch appeared as if years of weather and wind carved it out. Sandstone swirled around to form the bowl and reached up to connect to the towering Delicate Arch, where I was pulling my Spiderman moves, trying to hang on, hoping friction would be on my side.

I realized there was no going back up, because I would have to turn my body around and there was no place to do so. I would plummet. So I had to proceed forward. I had to descend into the bowl. The only problem was that it was a long and steep way down, and it looked nearly impossible to descent without a fall. If there were to be a fall it would be detrimental, for all of the ground was rock, and there was absolutely nothing to grab onto to break the fall. I would be sent rolling uncontrollably on the sandstone.

With wobbly legs and a queasy fear of the heights, I brought myself back onto two feet and immediately began my descent. I was running, trying to pair myself with gravity and avoid a complete fall. My feet stopped forcefully on the sandstone as I speedily propelled down into the bowl. My focus was staying on my feet and not falling out of control. With each passing second, as my feet stomped their way down into the bowl, I wasn't sure if I would remain standing. To quote a famous cowboy, Woody, you might say I was "falling with style." Despite my clumsiness I made it! I was in the rock bowl looking up at Delicate Arch, relieved, thankful to be unharmed, and gaining a view probably not too many people get to see of Delicate Arch.

When I first set out to explore around Delicate Arch I thought it was normal, but now judging the terrain, I knew this was not something people do. Furthermore, it was probably off limits. The last thing I needed was to get in trouble by the National Park Service, an organization I volunteer with and so admire. I needed to get back on the trail and blend in. I felt like an offender of the landscape. I was thoroughly embarrassed, knowing that my whole shenanigan was witnessed by dozens of tourists. Finding the trail involved hiking down into another bowl and climbing a much shorter distance up and out onto level land. Once back on the trail I felt like I needed to hike back to Delicate Arch and bid it farewell.

Thus was the extent of my main adventure in Arches National Park. The trail to Delicate Arch was one and a half miles and decently strenuous, working the calves and thighs as it is mostly an ascent on bare rock face. Near the trailhead there is a little off shoot trail that leads by some petroglyphs. I took it in on the way back and met a couple from Cincinnati, Ohio.

I overheard them talking about the horned looking monster in the petroglyph and how they noticed the same creature in the petroglyphs in Capitol Reef. "Aliens! They have to be aliens," the wife informed. Since I had just been to Capitol Reef I found it would be interesting to engage them in conversation. We talked petroglyphs and the nature of our trips, and they said they applauded me for venturing out on such a trip alone.

In addition to this main hike I also pulled over and

took the very quick hikes to Double Arch and Balanced Rock. At Double Arch I was recruited by a small group of Chinese tourist to take their picture. I was asked through a series of gestures, since we couldn't verbally communicate. Pointing at my camera and then myself I was able to get them to return the favor. This park was very busy and full of people from all over. I had noticed many tourists from China and Germany. Parking was very tricky but I was lucky.

Prior to arriving at the park, I had tuned into an AM radio station designated for the park, which was warning tourists that the park was expecting a large number of visitors and not to stop on the highway if the entrance to the park was backed up. I did not have this problem as I had

Double Arch

arrived fairly early in the morning. Once in the park boundary I ascended a large switchback road to higher ground
where I stopped at the visitor center. I watched the park
film and bought my customary pin. It was a very sleek and
modern visitor center. The park film spoke a lot about the
summer storms and how Delicate Arch was just one summer storm away from being broken and knocked down. It
made me speculate that perhaps in my lifetime Delicate
Arch would be no more, just like the fate of The Old Man
on the Mountain in New Hampshire, whom I visited as a
child but who no longer exists.

Also I decided to take care of my bookless dilemma
in the visitor center. I bought a 448 page book called The
American West by Dee Brown, a general history of the region, and I bought book about coyotes geared towards kids
but had a lot of great coyote pictures and facts that informed my purchase. Throughout my travels coyotes have
come to be my favorite animal, and I wanted to learn more
about them. Not being a bearer of a smartphone I relied on
old-fashion methods to gain my knowledge while traveling.

Just outside the visitor center there were two water
fill stations– spigots attached to pillars. Hikers gathered
around and lined up to fill their water bottles and hydration
packs. There was definitely a spirit of adventure in the air,
being surrounded by people with hydration packs and bottles of all shapes and sizes, all gearing up for their own explorations. I figured I should fill up on water as well, so I
brought over my Nalgene bottles and hydration packs and
became fully stocked up on water.

After Arches I headed into Moab, the nearest town and epicenter for outdoor adventure in Utah. This town is a major hub for the outdoor enthusiast. Everything is geared toward accommodating the adventurer. The town itself is very small. According to a 2016 census the population was 5,242, but the number of outdoor adventurers visiting is great and probably outnumbers the people living there. Although tourists were coming from all over the world to experience the wonders of Utah, bringing their own culture and customs, adventure and discovery bound us together, and because of that it was as if we all spoke a common language.

Balanced Rock

SEIZING THE MOMENT

"A whole month of camping! How do you stay clean?" This is a question I often get asked. There are a couple of answers I could give: I don't or let me tell you… I have gone for a week without a shower, but that is pretty much my max. I find ways, maybe not to stay clean, but to get clean from time to time when opportunity affords it. Most National Parks in the West do not have shower facilities, unless it's a largely popular National Park, then one might find a coin shower like in Bryce Canyon or Yellowstone. There's a very slim chance of finding a shower in a National Forest facility, as their standard is just a vault toilet and maybe, if you are lucky, a sink. Last year when I was camping in Sequoia National Park I counted a swim in a river enough of a bathe for me.

When no park shower facility is available I get creative. Often times I resort to getting a day pass to a gym and taking full advantage of the shower in the locker room. Gold's Gyms are popular throughout the West and a day pass is well worth it. For Moab I had to do a bit of prior investigation, but I did have a shower planned in my itinerary. Online I had found Moab's Recreation and Fitness Center. They expect visitors and charge solely for shower use, but they also offer a day pass to the gym. It has become my practice that if I'm going to shower at a gym, I'm going to get a good workout in too. As someone who is tall and lanky, with a fast metabolism, days on end of hiking cause me to lose muscle weight. I try to salvage some muscle by tearing it up in the gym and making sure I follow up with enough protein and nutrients to repair.

Moab's Recreation and Fitness facility was tucked away in the neighborhood in a very residential part of town. It was insightful to gain another perspective of Moab apart from the Main Street of tourist shops and restaurants. The neighborhood was clean, quiet, and simple. I parked alongside the road and went in to work out and get cleaned up. The facility was sleek and looked very new. The receptionist was very friendly.

When I work out in the gym I typically target one or two specific muscle groups. Since this was my first gym workout in a while, and would be the only one for days to come, I decided to work a little bit of everything.

When I'm back in Kentucky on normal time, I value lifting and working out in the gym for a multitude of reasons. One of them is that it keeps me physically fit to have these adventures. Pulling myself up and over rocks, climbing up steep slopes, hauling around large and heavy backpacks for miles, and the rare occurrence of holding onto a cliff edge for my life, requires that I have exceptional upper body strength. Also the self-discipline developed in the gym, allows me to keep pressing forward when things get difficult.

After my workout I was off to the shower. It felt absolutely amazing as the salty sweat, layers of sunscreen, and desert dust washed away from my face. I took in the comforting sensation of warm water relaxing my back, which had become so accustomed to being glued to a backpack.

Coming out of the shower, there were others moving in and out of the locker room, having just finished their own workouts. There were also kids having just finished swimming lessons going about in all directions. Wrapped in a towel, I laid my cinch bag on the counter next to the faucet and pulled out my shaving cream, razors, toothbrush, dental floss, and mouthwash. I had lots of personal maintenance work to be done. I felt rather awkward shaving in the midst of a bustling locker room. I remember when I lived in Houston, Texas people would shave in the locker rooms, but that was in a major city. Much more is acceptable in big cities than in small towns. I didn't know if this was socially acceptable here, but I went with it anyway. Even if people were to have passed silent judgment on me it didn't matter. They didn't understand how valuable this opportunity was for me, and plus, I was truly a stranger, here one day, gone the next. I would make sure I cleaned up after myself so what difference did it make?

When I left the recreation center I felt clean and refreshed. Evening was approaching. The sky was clear and the air was hot but dry. The harshness of the sun had receded. An overwhelming sense of peace met me in this moment. There is a certain sense of accomplishment obtained from being able to live out of a car and travel wherever you want . I remember returning feeling very pleased with life and myself. I felt ready and had amazing things planned and adventures to be had. I pulled from my food supply a Muscle Milk and a protein packed crispy rice bar.

Before heading to my campground I needed to run a few errands. I stopped by Walker Drug Company, which was a very impressive general store. It had a little bit of everything carefully and purposefully stocked: food, clothes, camping gear, souvenirs. In the East, the general store is pretty much nonexistent, except for the chain Dollar General. In the West, the independent general store is still alive. I bought one of my dietary staples, Greek yogurt, to get some additional protein after working out, and I purchased a dual prong USB charger for the car. I was impressed because I had never seen a dual prong USB charger. Later this would prove to be a nemesis, blowing a fuse in my car.

From the general store I went to City Market, Kroger rebranded for Utah. I was feeling sick of eating Clif Bars, jerky, and dried berries. I wanted some fresh food so I bought some apples, oranges, bananas, and peppers. After loading the groceries in my car, I was feeling hungry and also wanted to find some Wi-Fi to share the photo of myself by Delicate Arch. I stopped by a McDonalds. I got an Egg McMuffin (taking advantage of McDonald's new all day breakfast menu) and an iced coffee. I pulled out my Chromebook, inserted my SD card, and began searching for the photo of me next to the arch. This was a tedious task, as the machine was very slow, with it's memory at near full capacity from housing all my photos from last summer's adventure. While I was fumbling through the machine in search of the photo a young man, with hiking boots that were plastered with dusty Utah soil and a McDonalds tray in hand, took a seat right next to me. I looked over to see if he was going to say anything, but he said nothing. I found this very peculiar because the McDonald's was very spacious and numerous tables were open all over the place, but he chose to sit right next to me, our shoulders nearly touching. I could tell by his attire of cargo shorts, nylon t-shirt, and dusty boots that he had been out hiking. For a moment I thought about striking up conversation, but I was waiting for him to do so. After all, he is the one who rather awkwardly sat next to me, right inside my personal bubble.

My great fault of not taking initiative in meeting new people was on prime display here. I wanted to strike up conversation and hear his story. Was he another solo hiker by himself? What did we share in common? He didn't seem like he intentionally wanted to make me feel uncomfortable. He didn't seem very confident himself. It was as if he and I shared a lot in common. I imagine he had mustered up enough confidence to sit down next to a stranger but not enough to engage in step two: initiating a conversation. The social complex between us was very awkward. I felt that he innocently and sincerely saw himself in me and wanted to start a connection, but both of our social insecurities got the best of us. I just tucked my face away in my Chromebook and neither of us said anything.

Whenever I recall my experiences in Moab this comes to mind. If I had struck up conversation with him I wonder what would have become of the conversation. Would I have made a new friend? People sometimes misunderstand me and my solo adventures, thinking that I just want to be alone. Although I do enjoy some moments by myself, the reason why I adventure so often by myself is because there is no one else to share adventure with. Coming across another person who shares the same adventurous spirit, no matter who they are, is exciting to me. This young man in McDonald's could have been a valuable connection to share adventure stories with.

I can only conclude that this was a missed opportunity, and although I do believe everything happens for a reason, I think the takeaway from this is a lesson learned. From here on out I promised that if such an opportune situation for a social interaction comes my way I seize the moment and not let the opportunity pass.

Camping in Strange Woods

The sun had set but there was still enough light for me to barely see some of the wildlife around me. I passed nearly a dozen deer alongside the road. I was driving slowly, ascending an unknown mountain. An eerie unsettling sense of skepticism crept in. I was sixty miles removed from the bustle of Moab and just south of Canyonlands National Park. I had no framework to understand exactly where I was heading. I had a campsite reserved somewhere out here and had the coordinates entered in my GPS.

"You have reached your destination," my GPS cordially sounded. There was nothing there, so I continued on. After a few miles later up the mountain, I decided I better head back down and have another look. Sure enough, the second time I noticed my destination. There was a road. It was hard to see, and the entry onto it was through a cattle guard that had been nearly hidden with vegetation. Grass was growing up in the middle of it and vines were wrapping around it. Furthermore, the branches of the trees hung low and my vehicle would likely brush up against them. I eyed the passage for a moment. There was a sign "Buckboard Campground." This was it. The grate of the cattle guard was very wide. *Will my wheels get stuck on that?* I thought. There's only one way to find out. My car shook violently as it crossed the guard and shimmied through the tunnel of overgrowth. Then I was in.

There is no point in trying to recollect and recount my camping experience that night in the mountain, because in the intensity of the moment, I documented just what was going on:

Let it be documented that if there is ever a night I go strangely missing, it is tonight.

I am at Buckboard Campground in Utah. I found it impossible to find a campsite in Moab so I'm sixty miles south in Manti Lasal National Forest.

To arrive, I entered into the middle of nowhere and ascended thousands of feet into a thickly wooded forest of some sort of non-pine tree with a white trunk. I think they are aspen. I have never been in a white forest before. I'm sure in the morning light it is beautiful, but at night the unfamiliarity is eerie. The moon is super bright and it makes the trees look as if they are glowing.

Because this type of forest is new to me I don't know what dwells in these woods. Are there bears? I just bought a ton of produce, being sick of granola bars, dried nuts and berries, and jerky, and my sleeping bag smells like Subway. I bet my feet smell delicious too.

And I'm all alone. No one else is up here at this campground. So it is the perfect place to be kidnapped or snatched by Sasquatch, or Scarfinger, or the aliens in the petroglyphs I've seen today and yesterday. They may come to abduct me.

There are so many possibilities for my demise and disappearance. I'm trying to make light of the situation, but in all sincerity there is uneasiness and concern. I am completely isolated and alone in a strange place.

I quickly built a fire and turned on five flashlights, establishing my neck of the woods. And I tried to bear proof my car, but I'm simply carrying too much food. I am looking forward to sunrise. Please come soon.

Despite my trivial panic, I survived. To calm myself and make myself feel more at home I broke open my new book about the West and I became intrigued and lost in it's great story. I occasionally kicked the sides of my tent to create noise and scare off any campsite intruders, whenever I heard leaves ruffling. Despite my initial fear I slept very well.

I awoke the next morning in an absolutely beautiful aspen forest, and two deer nonchalantly walked right in front of my tent. I opened my tent window and talked to the deer for a moment. Tree trunks were vibrantly white and the leaves of the aspen created a glowing green canopy just above me. I fell in love with the aspen forest. I've been a huge fan of the aspen ever since.

Canyonlands and Dead Horses

One of the reasons why Canyonlands National Park is recollected with such fond memory is that the history here is real, apparent, exceptionally believable, and imaginable, as if one can reach out and touch it and bring it back to life. History is something that intrigues me, especially history of the West, of the Cowboys out on the plains with chuck wagons and cattle, pushing themselves to extremes, kicking up dust, and taking with every quench of thirst a side of desert grit; also the natives connecting with the land, battling their rivals in bloody encounters, carving their tales into the rocks around them, forming, creating, and leaving mysteries of their existence. Just days prior to visiting Canyonlands, I began reading the book *The American West*, and here in Canyonlands everything was put in its place, in scene, in context. I was here in the midst of what I was reading. These lands held the routes of the early cowboys, the homes of the Utes and Navajos. They ventured through this rough terrain and endured the harshness of the desert. Still to this day, surrounding the park on many sides are grasslands of cattle, modern day cowboys, and Native Americans blending tradition and culture.

When traveling from point A to point B, outside of the park, and pass over many cattle grates and plains stretching with herds, the West of cowboys and indians, which has often been elevated to the point of near folklore, is real, embraceable, and able to be experienced.

In my wanderings around Canyonlands, I took a short hike along a trail that passed by a rock overhang. In the shelter of the overhang was equipment and items left by cowboys of the past, including tables, trunks, saddles, cups and cans. I remember in that moment I paused and I tried to imagine the transient life of the cowboy out in these harsh canyonlands of intense arid heat. The amount of bravery and perseverance of cowboys is admirable.

Just next to the boundary of Canyonlands National Park is Dead Horse Point State Park. Here I took a morning jog along the canyon rim, which ended right at the overlook of Dead Horse Point itself. In front of me was a wild expanse of canyons and an elevated peninsula where the Green River dramatically curves around. The air was dry but the desert was not yet sweltering. Everything around me was painted in vibrant shades or orange, red, and pink. When I was done admiring the scene I went into the visitor center. "So tell me, what's with the name Dead Horse?" I asked.

The park employee gladly explained, "Cowboys traveled long distances out in the desert with little water. They were very thirsty and their horses even more so. They followed the sound of the river to the outcropping of land you see at the bend of the river. When they arrived, there they stood right next to the river but far above it. They could see it and hear it but had no way to get down to it, and so their horses died thirsty, looking at the unreachable river."

In the gift shop I bought a book titled *Down the Great Unknown: John Wesley Powell's 1869 Journey of Discovery and Tragedy Through the Grand Canyon* by Edward Dolnick. The employee informed me that there was the John Wesley Powell River History Museum not far away. Unfortunately I didn't have the time to visit.

Although I had debated even stopping at Dead Horse Point State Park I am glad I did. It compliments Canyonlands National Park and the views of the Canyonlands and Dead Horse Point were alluring and picturesque views. Something very unique about this region is you have Arches National Park, Canyonlands National Park, Dead Horse State Park, and numerous other parks and natural features all in close proximity of Moab being the hub in the middle.

Back in the National Park I didn't see much during the day. I was out on a small trail of barren rock faces taking photos over at the beautiful spiky rock formations in the Needles District when an angry looking storm came rolling it. I could see it moving, and see the sheets of rain it carried and the bolts of lightning it sent snapping to the ground. In this moment the sky and scenery were perfect for photo tak-

ing, but some dust was stuck in my camera lens and I realized the approaching danger of the storm. I quickly satisfied
my need to take photos with a few good shots and returned
to my car just in time before the downpour. In the West
storms are much more frightening with the knowledge that
water is not soaked into the land and there is rarely anything
taller than your vehicle. So you and your car stand out, exposed for the storms and all its bouts of lightning. With
what I'm used to, a car provides adequate shelter from a
storm, but not in these parts. I retreated to more trustwor-
thy shelter in the visitor center.

When I was at Arches National Park, just days prior,
I had heard about the summer storms in the park film,
which have threatened some of the arches in the park, but I
had no way to fully understand them. The land seemed so
dry and the sky unyielding to any clouds. Trying to imagine

a storm in these parts was difficult. Now in the midst of one, it was completely understood. But like all summer storms on these barren planes and canyonlands, it didn't last long. It came and went, in a quick heated tantrum.

Canyonlands National Park is composed of three districts, each with unique lands features. There is the Island in the Sky District, the Needles District, and the Maze District. In the visitor center at the Island in the Sky District, I inquired about hiking down into the Needles District I had seen from my former hike. The park ranger took out a white binder with photos slid into plastic sleeves. He turned to a specific page and pointed to it. "Well this is the Needles District." He paused for a moment, as if the photo itself would be a deterrent. It wasn't. It looked amazing. "There is no cell phone service out there…" *Fine with me.* He proceeded, "…and GPS devices won't work in that area from the rocks blocking the signals." His last piece of information successfully deterred me from exploring the area. I had read online that it was ill-advised to go alone, as all the rock formations which stick up like needles create a maze-like environment, and it's very easy to get lost. It was advised that one takes pictures at turning points in the trail to be able to navigate back to the starting point. That knowledge paired with the fact that my GPS would not work, resulted in the decision to not explore the Needles District. I had already been hiking in the area enough to know the arid heat was a serious thing. Being lost here could be deadly, and I didn't want to end up like the horses of Dead Horse Point.

When the rain had subsided I made it to Mesa Arch-the most iconic feature in the park. It's a small rock arch right on the edge of a canyon cliff. It's not much taller than myself but what makes it so appealing is that it frames the canyonlands behind it perfectly and is positioned at just the right angle for sunlight to bring out vibrant color in the landscape, making this location an exceptionally good photo spot at sunrise and sunset. Now, after having visited Mesa Arch, I notice it frequently in screensavers, calendars, and different pieces of publicity. While I was there a group of young adults from France asked me to take their picture. I had seen them the day before in Arches National Park. There was a small crowd of people gathering, but everyone was very respectful, stepping aside for each other to take pictures with the arch.

At one point in my day I took a break and went into Moab for lunch. I ate at the Moab Diner, which was a very pleasant experience. I would recommend it to anyone in the

area. Not only was the food delicious but the service was unparalleled. The waiters were extremely attentive, and I must have had my glass of water refilled at least five times. I had gotten the Kokopelli Chicken Sandwich. It was here I made the association that Kokopelli is the flute player in the petroglyphs. His image is reproduced all over merchandise and signage in the area. He is a fertility deity and represents the spirit of music. I don't know much else about Kokopelli except his chicken sandwich was delectable.

Nearing the end of the day I returned to Canyonlands to walk to Grand View Point at sunset. This walk would prove to be a pinnacle of self-actualization and discovery on this trip, and will be outlined in my next chapter, but after my hike along the rim I began driving back to my hideout in the mountains of Manti Lasal. Shortly outside the park I drove by a Bureau of Land Management sign for Horse Thief Campground. Weary from a full days adventure I thought I would check it out and entertain the idea of camping here instead. Sure enough there were campsites available. I decided I'd rather dish out fifteen dollars then drive sixty more miles in the dark back to Manti Lasal. Alt-

Mesa Arch

hough my tent was all set up in Manti Lasal, I had my spar tent, Kelty, and an extra sleeping bag in my car. I also had one of my compact camping pillows. I would be alright. I sent up camp there in the flat exposed plain. The sky above me was extremely huge. Clouds were long gone now, and stars filled the sky. I was able to purchase some firewood on the grounds and quickly had a small fire blazing. I was camping, like the cowboys I read about, out on the expansive plains, with the vast star-studded sky above me.

I realized here that I could position a flashlight underneath my glow-in-the-dark Nalgene bottle, and the bottle would disperse the light creating a calm but sufficient glow by which I could see to eat a snack and write a few postcards. When my writing was complete, and the air grew cool and hollow, I crawled into my airy tent, pulled out my book on the West, and read to the sound and glow of the fire next to me and the brightness of the unhindered moon and stars above me. I was at peace.

THE CANYONS IN MY LIFE

I looked down over an expanse and saw a whole different world. Perched on its edge, I knew that it would only be a matter of time before I would explore its grand expanse and profound depths. For now the vista in front of me was so massive and colorful that my mind couldn't take it all in, but I could admire the thousand shades of color, from rich red, to golden orange, pale brown, and deep purple. I entertained thoughts concerning the world below me, all the different nooks and crannies, all the different river ways, and the solitary towers of rock leaving islands in the sky. I could conjure up stories of adventure in the depths and speculate the history of people living in and passing through the narrows. Canyons are rich for the imagination and profound for inspiration.

At just around sunset I started this hike along the

canyon rim at Canyonlands National Park. It had been a full day of hiking many trails and covering many miles. I felt accomplished but I was getting tired and I wanted time to wind down, so just a leisurely stroll along the canyon rim at sunset seemed perfect.

When I go hiking I always end up taking away more than I can imagine, nothing physical but rather inspiration, reassurance, and healing. Nature has a way of bringing about these things, and I've lived enough life to know that nature itself is not some mystical magical entity, but rather I believe nature is a creation designed purposefully to appeal to man and take him to depths of self-actualization and to intimacy with God. Often times when I go hiking alone I find it to be the perfect time to pause, reflect, and just be in the presence of God. Out in the solace of His natural beauty it's sometimes easier to hear God speak. I have seen this evident in my own life in many instances. God uses natural beauty to speak to me. The rocks, the trees, the towering mountains, and canyon depths are designed to have meaning. They are symbols.

As I was hiking along that rim I was reflecting on my life, trying to pinpoint where exactly in my life I was feeling a corrosive emptiness and deficit, despite my fleeting feelings of accomplishment. I was pouring out to God this discontentment and feeling of inadequacy. This was something that had plagued me for a while. I felt I was just not doing something right, that I wasn't living up to my potential, and my character was lacking something.

While I was feeling these heavy emotions the sun

was hidden behind a cloud, and therefore the countless canyons of Canyonlands were dark, mysterious, and seemingly bottomless. Lines separating the sections of the canyon were blurred from lack of sunlight. In this moment, suddenly it hit me, the realization that my own life has a number of canyons– deep and dark places where light just doesn't shine, where the lines are blurred. I wasn't sure exactly what those canyons were and what was the cause of them, but I knew there were dark places in my life where lines that separate truth from lies had been blurred, places that were corrosive that continued to grow deeper and darker. I asked God to show me the canyons in my life.

Canyons are very interesting things in relation to life. They are cavities in the earth's surface caused by erosion over time. They are huge but can begin forming by something so simple as just a crack. Water eats away and erodes the trivial into something massive. However other times the impetus for formation is the land itself shifting as plates collide and move. And so the dark places in our lives can form very much like canyons. They may start as something trivial on the surface, a seemingly harmless sin, which over time can erode a person's life. Sometimes those cracks we aren't even responsible for, but they are caused by the abuse of others which start to erode our very being. Other times these canyons are formed by major life events, with loss or dramatic changes, when we feel the earth is pulled right out from under us.

As I was reflecting on canyons and their relevance to life, inspired by all the metaphors I could apply to life, suddenly the sun broke through an opening in the clouds. Beams of warm yellow light shot down and reached a number of canyons. The beams of light were situated at just the right angles that they illuminated the deepest canyons. And just like that a number of dark and dreary canyons became strikingly beautiful and awesome, no longer dreary and dark but rich in color and light.

At this moment God spoke to me, not in any audible voice but rather more directly, right to my soul. He told me that he can take the canyons in my life and turn them into something beautiful. Tears began to roll down my face in response to the beautiful parallels God was making and hearing His voice, which had seemed absent in my life for quite some time.

My first response was thankfulness, thankful that God met me here, literally out wandering in the desert. Secondly, I began searching my life for canyons. That evening I wasn't sure of the canyons in my life but I was ready to face them. I was inspired to seek change in my life and let God illuminate those dark places in my life.

Since this evening I have been able to identify some canyons in my life. I know one of my most profound canyons is selfishness, which is a complex and sprawling canyon. I am still on a quest to find the rest of my canyons, confront them, and let God's light transform them into something beautiful. I love how God is transformative and resourceful. He doesn't let bad experiences and choices in life exist without redemption. God uses the dark places in our lives and illuminates them to bring him glory and fulfill his purpose.

I encourage everyone to take a hike out in nature and talk to God and ask Him to show you your own canyons. I am uncertain of all my canyons but I know God will lead me to them, and he can lead you to yours too.

Try this whether you have faith in God or not. Just go out in nature and reflect on the places in life you need to work on to be a better you— the "canyons". I pray that on your quest to find your canyons you encounter God, because I'm telling you, there's nothing more powerful.

Exploring the Uncharted

"There are no maps of that area," she informed. "I keep asking them to make maps, but I work for the government. We can never get anything done. It's basically uncharted area, but you are welcome to explore."

I had stopped by a small visitor center in Monticello, Utah next to the mountains of Manti Lasal National Forest. When I had camped up in the mountains two nights before, in the aspen forest, I had noticed some trails off to the side of the road. Surely the visitor center would have some maps, I thought. I was wrong.

She kept repeating herself and was very apologetic. I was a little disappointed until the words "uncharted area" sunk into my mind, and I realized that this was a prime and rare opportunity to explore.

"Thank you," I replied, walking outside with a skip in

my step. I was on the brink of some serious adventure, about to take on uncharted area.

I drove up into the mountains, pulled over, and parked by the lake I sat by to have breakfast the day before. There was a gate open to the gravel driveway. I made sure to park by the side of the road before passing through the gate. I was by no means in a parking spot, but I hadn't seen a single vehicle up here. I felt pretty confident that my vehicle would be fine.

Unsure of what to expect I applied mosquito repellent, filled up my hydration pack, and packed away a Clif bar and a long sleeve shirt. I turned on my GPS, walked down alongside the road about a fourth of a mile, and began one of my favorite hikes ever!

It started out as a wide unmarked trail that had clearly been used for four-wheeler ATVs. The path at times dipped down into ruts from tires. Trees were sparse at first. Rock and grass dominated the landscape. The sun was bright and the path was dusty, painting into my memory a landscape of bright warm yellow. Then my memories turn into rich greens and the vibrant white of a young aspen forest. I was fully intrigued. I had been hiking in many types of forests before— in the pine forest of the northeast and the Sierra Nevada of the West, the subtropical forest of Kentucky and Tennessee, down to the tropics of Florida, but I had never been in an aspen forest.

As silly as it may sound to those so accustomed to aspen, to me it was like stepping into another world. I thought I knew the forest. I thought I knew trees, but here

I was with my concept of a forest challenged and expanded. It was an entirely different environment than anything I had ever seen before. I had camped in an aspen forest two nights prior but it was different to be hiking out in one, noticing the forest floor fully green and covered with thick wispy grass. The branches of the aspen wait to sprout towards the top of the tree, leaving the hikers range of view immense with a seemingly endless display of tree trunks congregated together.

There was something very calming, comforting, and strangely eerie about the aspen forest. Although I am a fan of all types of forest, typically the forests I venture into have a certain sense of expected mystery about them, because dark, large trunks, obtrusive branches, and wild undergrowth keep secrets and stories hidden. Typically my view in the forest is limited, for there is so much space for things to be out of sight. But the aspen forest is different. It's very open. The forest floor is one sheet of wispy grass Everything is visible around these slender trunks and nothing is hidden and mysterious. Instead bright and cheerful trunks invite your into the gathering, accepting you as one of the party, but after making acquaintance, and being invited inside, the trees at times can seem like pale white ghosts, only a mirage of a true forest. But then you stop, and this is when you listen to their millions of small leaves rattle against each other and sing, telling you that they are alive.

This particular forest I was exploring was young so the Aspen's weren't very tall, giving me a larger than life feeling. I felt almost like a giant trampling through a world of my own. I stopped here at the beginning of the aspen forest for maybe a good twenty minutes, captivated by the trees.

There is something extremely pleasing and satisfying to me in discovering new terrains. Every different type of terrain I explore challenges and expands my perception of the world. I recall my first experience in a forest of palm trees, walking out on desert a plain for the first time, gazing through the ponderosa pines of Yosemite, and looking down into canyon depths. Every time I experience a new type of terrain the richness of my life increases. It opens new pathways in my mind to ponder and explore in memory and imagination. It shows me the diverse nature of the creativity of God, and I am simply swept away in bliss-ful wonder and enjoyment.

After my impromptu visit with the aspen I returned to the trail and decided to pick up the pace. The trail even-tually came to a fork. It was my goal to summit the moun-tain before me. There was a sign, and I chose the direction with the name that sounded more like a summit of a moun-tain to me. I chose the path to my left. Clearly ATV time was over for this path was much smaller. I followed along-side the sound of a stream, which I never could see. It was down in a ravine.

Shortly the forest changed. Tall older aspen mixed with robust ancient pines. Eventually the aspen were left behind and I was in the company of dark, rich, wet pines. The smell was sweet, tremendously pleasing. It smelled like fond memories of Christmas, and soon enough I found snow to accompany the sweet aroma. A mound of snow rose up mid trail. I was so excited to come upon it. So far on my trip I had been venturing in dry hot desert, even just this morning I was trekking along the red hot rock of Canyonlands National Park. Now here I was in a cool, aromatic pine forest, climbing up a pile of snow. I took snow into my hands and threw icy snowballs into the forest.

I felt like I had jumped from summer into winter in the matter of an hour– and not into any gloomy bitter wintertime, but a festive, picturesque, quintessential Christmasland of sorts.

I checked my GPS. Time was ticking. I was five miles in. Time and distance had passed so quickly. The day was by no means young anymore. Evening was upon me. Because I had no map, no insight to these trails, I was unsure where exactly this trail was leading. I couldn't gage if it would lead to a summit or simply meander around the mountains. I also considered that everything I hiked had to be re-traced, and I did not want to be stuck in uncharted wilderness in the dark. I had a resolution. I would pick up the pace, run through the forest, and at every mile I would reassess the situation.

My blissful run through the pine forest took me to an alpine tundra. Trees were left behind and tundra prairie spread across the mountain. The trail was but a narrow pathway making steep inclines up the mountain. Around me I looked down to dramatic valleys and ravines, with tall pines looking as tiny figures. The excitement propelled me forward at incredible pace.

Around me, every so often, Utah prairie dogs poked their heads out of their burrows as if to check to see if the world around them was still present. I ran past them leaving the trail behind me to summit the top of the world. Reaching the mountaintop was a grand climax as I could look out and see the cavities of Canyonlands as a miniature little wonderland below. I was on the cool green tundra looking down into the hot dry desert. The contrast was remarkable. A small cluster of pine trees huddled together just near the summit, pointing to the sky, but also further drawing out the stark contrast of the pine forest and the beautiful canvas of Canyonlands in the background.

What made this moment all the more exciting and special to me was that I felt like I had truly discovered this place. There were no tourists, no signage, no constructed platforms nor overlooks. It was truly wild, and secret, and entirely a new experience for me.

It would have been enjoyable to have spent more time up here looking around and taking in the scenery, maybe sitting down and enjoying a moment of quietude, but I knew there wasn't much time to spare since I was eight miles up a mountain and wanted to get back before dark.

I stood atop that mountain feeling powerful, invigorated, and accomplished. Then I turned around and ran back down. I was pleased. I had done it. When I set out on the path I wasn't sure where I was going, and then as I ascended I knew I was getting closer to the top. Doubt had set in a few times. I was wondering if I would be able to make it to the summit. But I did and the view, not only on the top, but on all my journey to the top was most rewarding.

This mountain and this Aspen forest continue to linger in my mind. It's a place I couldn't easily direct anyone to. It's mine. It's my secret. My cherished memory. I've tried looking at a map and identifying exactly what mountain I summited but it's unclear, so it remains only a place I can describe, only a place I understand, and my hike up that mountain was so full of adventure and wonder that it almost seems like a dream— a moment I escaped reality and pulled myself from the limited view of the world to look down on it with grateful solitude and awe.

Hiking on trails alone, as on this one, has never given rise to feelings of loneliness. Although I've at times wanted to share beautiful vistas and moments with people, I've never been overwhelmed with loneliness. Instead these moments of solitude remind me that in our lives we all walk a path no one else has trodden. No one will fully understand and no one can ever recount my journey but myself and the One who created me. For each life is uniquely different, made up of different experiences filtered through our own unique perceptions. I imagine that even in companionship, complete and true understanding of my life, despite how close one may be, can never be reached, for we are limited by our human capabilities. But God knows truly what it is like to walk my path. He has been and is with me the entire way. So in these moments, when I hike alone, I find incredible intimacy with God and comfort in knowing that, even

though no one else can fully understand the life I lead, my
path in life is not walked alone. He knows it completely, before the dawn of my existence all the way to the end of my
days, and He is with my every step in the present to assure
me purpose and understanding. In that I find peace.

That evening I quickly ran eight miles down the
mountain, speeding like Sonic the Hedgehog. Back at my
car I checked my GPS to log the numbers of miles hiked. I
was excited to add sixteen miles to the tally. I then turned
my car around and went back to Buckboard Campground.
Two days prior it was a strange forest to me, but now it was
pleasantly understood. I could find comfort in it, my secret
aspen hideaway in the mountains. I crawled into True Blue,
pulled out my book on the West, and shortly drifted to
sleep.

Canyons too Deep

When considering Canyons and their relevance to life a moment in Canyonlands National Park comes back to me, when in the visitor center the ranger said the canyon was too deep and the walls too high for the GPS signal to reach down.

I have explored, in my thoughts and writing, how in our lives there can be canyons— places we let get out of control, places of our wrongful choices, our hurt, our pain, which continue to decay, growing dark and deep. But I've mentioned how those places are not beyond redemptive reach. The light of God can reach down into those places in our lives and bring about beauty from the darkness. He can bring restoration and healing. He can even take our canyons and build up mountains. He can turn our weaknesses into unwavering strengths.

But what about a canyon so dark and deep that the

signal just doesn't reach down? It's blocked because the walls are so deep and are closing in on you. To me this is a fascinating concept. I know in my life I've come across people who have felt this way. They feel their choices in life have defiled and defined them and put them beyond the reach of God. First off, they are wrong. I believe physically and spiritually "neither height nor depth, nor anything else in all creation, will be able to separate us from the love of God that is in Christ Jesus our Lord." - Romans 8:39. God pursues us and reaches his hand down to pull us out of these dark places.

However, despite the hope that there always is in God, when the canyon walls are growing tall we need to consider this a warning and consider those around us. Often there are people in our lives to help us— family and friends, and even people out of the blue, but if we harden our hearts and don't let these people help we lose their signals. If we resist them and don't let them help us out of our canyons they give up on us, and we find ourselves in a deep state of solitude and desperation.

I know particularly those who embrace drugs and affairs often resist the signals sent by the ones closest to them. Their hearts become hardened and callous, and the signals do not reach them. Their canyons grow dark and deep until I'm sure for them it seems there is no way out. Sometimes it feels like there's nothing we can do further to help the people in these situations but leave them to their own demise.

Despite his ability to help us, God too will leave us

alone in our canyons if that is our desire. It's said in the scripture a number of times that God hands people over to their evil desires. But at the same time, God's hand is still there reaching out for us to bring us back. His knowledge surpasses all understanding and his signals reach down into our deepest canyons. We just have to receive them. He is the only one that won't abandon us when sometimes everyone else will. He is there, and it all comes down to a choice to reach out to him, receive those signals, or stay put in the deep dark canyon.

When you reach out your hand and send signals to someone you love in a dark place, and despite all your efforts your message is rejected, blocked out from the canyon, this hurts. It's enough to form a crack in your heart, a place for a canyon of self-doubt to grow. You begin to doubt your ability to help others, and you feel hopelessness in the situation. Although you sought to help someone out of a canyon you ultimately find yourself in a canyon that erodes into distrust, distrusting God's sovereignty in the situation.

I can't imagine what it's like for those in very close family relations when signals aren't accepted and efforts are given up. People are left having to watch their loved ones descend further into darkness. There has to be immense pain and even anger seeing these people hike deeper into their canyons. In such situations, at the end of the day, we all have to rely on God, knowing that He truly is sovereign and His ability to lift these people out of their canyons is never gone. We need to lay our worries on Him and trust that nothing goes past His watch.

In the midst of this, find peace in following a blameless path. Despite signals being rejected, be persistent, offering help numerous times. But if all of your efforts are disregarded, step back, hold no guilt nor responsibility, knowing you offered your best. Come to terms with the fact that this canyon you find your loved one in is not your canyon but it was his or her choice. At the same time, follow the example set to us by God. If this person ever reaches out their hand to you, take hold and help them out.

Some do have to be careful, when they extend their hands down into a canyon to help others because some canyons block judgment, darken hearts, and bring about malice. The people in these canyons may tug at your reach to bring you down into their canyons with them. It's important to have an unwavering stance on the higher ground, for a crippled man cannot help his neighbor walk.

As I reach out into canyons of darkness to offer my help and its not accepted, I perhaps feel a small fragment of pain God feels when He looks upon His creation that He loves so much as they reject Him and stay put in their canyons when there are mountains to be raised.

Look around, are their canyon walls closing in around you? Are there people around you who love you who are sending you signals? Are they being used as instruments of a higher power? Know that in all the confusion and darkness there is a light brighter than anything this world has to offer that will reach into your canyon and illuminate it.

Perhaps you are on a plateau or a mountain side and

you are reaching back down to help others out of their own canyons, but they refuse to accept your help. Despite the hurt you feel, leave your arm extended. Have your hand available to grab onto. Seek peace in your own life. Don't lose hope that maybe someday you will feel their hands of humility grasp onto yours.

ARRIVING AT BLACK CANYON

Something was wrong, and I wasn't quite sure what it was. I noticed the hubcaps on my rental car looked warped and out of place. *I shouldn't have gone on those rough roads in Saguaro and Capitol Reef,* I thought. I've knocked the hubcaps out of place. This had been on my mind for a few days, but there was nothing I could do about it until now. I was finally amidst real civilization. I was in Grand Junction, Colorado with all the amenities of corporate America at my fingertips. I pulled up to a Walmart Auto Care Center to inquire about my hubcaps.

"Can you just have a look and tell me what's wrong." I guided the mechanic across the parking lot to my car.

"Oh, well they were put on wrong in the first place." He informed. He peeled the hubcaps away from the rims of the wheels. "You should be fine now." I was relieved that it was an easy fix and to see normal looking hubcaps again. I thanked the man and went into the Walmart to stock up on supplies. I felt I owed them a purchase. Just prior I had eaten at a Del Taco, one of my go-to places when venturing out West. Those in the rest of the country wouldn't know that a Del Taco is like a step above a Taco Bell, with fresher ingredients and more healthy and filling options, with fresh avocados and tomatoes. I sound like an advertising spokesperson when I talk about them, but I'm just a fan.

Prior to rolling into Grand Junction I had left Manti Lasal National Forest in Utah and had driven about two hours from Utah into Colorado. I had stopped to visit Colorado National Monument which largely sits high on a mountainous plateau of red rock looking down across flatlands of Colorado. I didn't have much time to spare but checked out a few view spots, including the popular Coke Ovens, which are large rounded rock formations that stick up in a row in a canyon.

In my planning of these summer adventures I recall being first confused about what a National Monument was. In my mind a monument was a statue or some mounted object in honor of a specific event. This is not what a National Monument is. Rather they are very similar to National Parks. Most National Parks first start out as National Monuments. I once inquired about this to a park ranger. He explained that really the only difference is that a National Monument is a park unit created by a president, and a National Park is a unit created by an act of Congress. The major difference between the two is that National Parks tend to gain more tourism simply because of the title.

The Coke Ovens

Colorado National Monument was my first ever impression of Colorado. I had seen photos of the Rocky Mountains and the Maroon Bells of Colorado, and I was heavily influenced by the pine trees, grey rocks, and snow-capped mountains. I was surprised to find so much red rock in Colorado. However, being here it just made sense, given that it lies right next to the red rock wonderland of Utah. Despite seeing beautiful photos of Colorado online, I had read several negative things about Colorado in the wake of political agendas

Despite my preconceived notions, Colorado was surprising all around. It borrows from that which is beautiful in Utah but adds in its own unique natural beauty. It has more people than Utah, with more frequent towns and cities and less feelings of isolation, with a population at 5.54 million, nearly doubling that of Utah. After visiting Colorado National Monument I descended into the city of Grand Junction, Colorado, with population around 61,000. The part of the city I saw appeared new and clean with wide and smooth properly constructed streets.

After spending days in remote areas I always become so very appreciative of places like Grand Junction. Although in the course of typical life-living, supermarkets, fast food, restaurants, air conditioning, and all the amenities of modern America become common place and stale, when I've been isolated from them for days and I come upon them again, it is genuinely exciting. In the moment there seems to be nothing better than feeling the brisk air conditioning, to feel the refreshing coldness of ice in my beverage and an unlimited supply of cold water, to find food already prepared and available in bounty. The ease and accessibility of all of these goods is made possible by corporate America, which is something to be grateful for. These businesses, despite recently being attacked, labeled, and stereotyped, provide incredible service, and are only possible in this great nation. Getting away and spending time in nature helps me become more appreciative of the simplicities of modern life that we enjoy and are so fortunate to have in these United States.

After having the hubcaps on the car adjusted, dining at Del Taco, and restocking on food at Walmart, I was ready to proceed as planned with the day's agenda– to shower and workout in Montrose, set up camp, and do a little sightseeing in Black Canyon of the Gunnison National Park.

The drive took me through the small town of Delta, which to me felt like stepping back in time to an era I wasn't even alive to witness. Although it was a quiet place, its main street had many businesses, not for tourism, but simply placed ordinarily with vintage looking facades. There was a general store, a fabric store, a jewelry shop, a small grocery store, and numerous little Mexican restaurants. Here I felt far away. The uniqueness and old timey feel made me aware of the distance I had traveled.

I proceeded into Montrose where I purchased a day pass to the Gold's Gym. I was surprised that such a large and nice gym was located in such a small town. As I was working out, doing a little bit of everything, I observed the locals around me, wondering what life might be like for them and wondering what they might do for work. I'm sure I didn't stick out and that I blended in as just another guy at the gym. As they were doing their typical gym routines, going about ordinary life, here I was on an epic adventure, just paused for a moment in this small seemingly insignificant town, which really drew me to it for only one reason— a gym with a shower.

After my workout and shower, I dug into my food supply in my trunk and enjoyed a cinnamon raisin bagel and a Muscle Milk. I followed it up with a grilled chicken wrap at the nearby McDonalds. I sat there in McDonalds and for a moment I did feel a bit of loneliness. I remembered the lost opportunity to connect with the other solo adventurer at the McDonalds in Moab. I saw a family on the other side of the restaurant eating together. I wasn't in some major touristy spot where I could relate to the gamut of people around me on adventures. I was in a small town. People were about ordinary life. I thought of many times I had tried to form friendships and relationships with people, but how they sometimes bailed out on me. I thought about how long I had waited for people to go on adventures with and the reason I found myself out here alone was because I became tired of waiting and decided to move on alone. I thought about how all the incredible memories made would be mine and no one else could recollect them with me. I also thought about how all efforts to connect with people were not completely lost. There were my postcard buddies I had been writing. My two postcard buddies were new people to me. I wondered would this effort to connect with them be fruitful or was it all done in vain?

Then I came back to my senses. I didn't come all the way out to Colorado to sit in a McDonalds and feel sorry for myself. To make it out here alone, seeing so many beautiful places, and finding my way so effortlessly was an accomplishment of independence and something to be proud of. I picked myself off of that plastic McDonalds booth, emptied my tray into the trash, and then it was onward to Black Canyon of the Gunnison.

Approaching the park it was really hard to anticipate anything, because the terrain and the small town surrounding it were just so typical. But rather suddenly I came upon a giant break in the terrain, an enormous open wound in the landscape. A dark ominous gap dug sharply into the ground. I realized Colorado has surprises.

I have mixed feelings about this National Park. The canyon itself is surely impressive. There is nothing I have seen quite like it. It is a very dramatic canyon with very sharp edges and rocks pointing and jutting up from it. The rock looked as if it had been violently chopped to carve the canyon. Standing by it and looking into it I received the kind of awe I might encounter if I were to gaze upon the fictitious castle of a vile king. It is beautiful if you take the time to admire all its special peculiarities, but at first glance it looks rather uninviting. It's not inspiring to me. It's not like looking up at a mountain and losing yourself in the beauty of the moment. Black Canyon seems more like a warning from the forces of nature, a display of its violent ability. It's dark, sharp, gaping, and hollow.

Prior to my trip I had entertained the idea of hiking down into the canyon to greet the Gunnison River, but I had read too many warnings of poison ivy overgrowth and how the descent is not much of a trail but a free for all which at parts require the hiker to lower himself by holding onto ropes and traversing the steep slopes of the canyon walls. I had not ruled out the possibility of descending into the canyon, but when I looked at it I came to a conclusion. Sometimes I'll see a mountain and have the nagging desire to summit it, like in Manti Lasal, but there was little to no desire to put myself at risk to place myself into a dark and ominous abyss.

"Will you take our photo," a man asked me while I was looking over the edge into the depths.

"Sure," I snapped the photo.

"Let me do the same for you," the man offered to return the favor.

"No, it's okay." I replied.

"Oh come on, you need a picture," He insisted. He struck me as very friendly. He took my photo and it came out really well. I noticed his hat sported an Indiana school. I had to ask him where he came from. He was from Indiana. When he asked me where I was from, I claimed Kentucky.

I proceeded further into the park to the visitor center. The park film was chock full of lots of interesting history about the canyon. This provided much more richness to my Black Canyon experience. I learned how the canyon was largely avoided until the 1900s. It's river waters were so violent that wooden boats were turned to splinters by explorers. One successful survey of the canyon was done by a couple of men floating on a mattress. Also the history of a railroad stretching along the sides of the canyon and the effort that went into constructing it was incredible.

History here is rich, but I was surprised to find this place bared the title National Park. National Parks to me usually boast numerous features and plenty of opportunity for recreation. This park is small. There aren't many trails, and the different features seem to be limited to view spots at just various angles of the same canyon and river. It seems unjust to place it in the same category as places like Yosemite or the Great Smoky Mountains or any National Park I had visited up until this point.

After squeezing in my stop at the visitor center before it closed, I backtracked a little bit on the road to set up
camp at the South Rim campground. The terrain was part
woodsy, part deserty. I wasn't sure what animals might be
around at night. Ever since I visited Sequoia National Park
and was warned about black bears breaking into cars I have

become extra careful not to leave food items out in my vehicle. My campsite, which I had reserved online, was very private. The fire ring and picnic tables were in an open exposed area but behind a row of tall shrubbery was a place to set up the tent, completely shielded on all sides by growth. I quickly pitched True Blue and continued on the park drive, stopping at numerous viewpoints.

The two most notable view spots for me were Pulpit Rock, where long ago a minister used this rock to deliver sermons to his congregation, also Painted Wall, which is a section of dark rock with bright white stripes running through it. This is another geological landmark I hadn't noticed before, but afterward have seen it in ads and billboards. I had all intentions of being at Warner Point for sunset, seeing that right next to it on the map is labeled "Sunset View," but again I was moments late for the sunset. It was okay. I was tired and what I wanted most of all at this moment was a good night's sleep.

I returned to my campsite in the dark, got ready for bed, and without reading, without thoughts to ponder, I flipped my switch and fell asleep.

The Painted Wall

STAR-STRUCK AT ROCKY MOUNTAIN NATIONAL PARK

"There's a moose on the road!" the lady exclaimed.

There are no moose in the Rocky Mountains of Colorado, I thought.

"Just up ahead on the road you'll see him."

Poor lady, I thought. She doesn't know the difference between a moose and an elk.

However, in my ignorance I was wrong. She was right.

I had just gotten out of my car at the Kawuneeche Visitor Center in Rocky Mountain National Park. I had been arriving from the West via Grand Lake. She had been arriving from the East. Apparently there was a moose on the road up ahead, but I missed it and stopped at the visitor center. I didn't bother asking about hiking trails. I had done my research online and knew what I wanted to do, and I was very excited about it. This was the Rocky Mountain National

Park! It's one of those rare places you hear so much about and can't believe you are actually there when you arrive.

For me Rocky Mountain National Park stands in a prestige collection of National Parks. Some National Parks just certainly have more fame than others. This was one of the big ones. I'd file it along with Yosemite, Yellowstone, Glacier, and the Great Smoky Mountains. I made sure before arriving I had planned out this visit. I needed to be assured that my Rocky Mountain experience would be full and complete. I didn't want to miss anything. I felt my plan was solid. And here, meeting Rocky Mountain National Park was like meeting a very famous celebrity. There was sure excitement, a bit of nervousness, and the whole fascination from being starstruck.

Leaving the visitor center I made my way on the park road to the alpine summit. Along the way I made a few stops. I had gotten out of my car at Coyote Valley to gaze across the Kawuneeche Valley where meadows of green grass were adorned with clusters of pine. Along the valley edges the terrain gradually rises and stretches. It grows with thickening dark pine forest until it can reach no further and mountaintops peak with barren rocky tops capped in snow.

Next to me, just meandering right through the meadow grass, at level with the rest of the ground, was the Colorado River. It looked like nothing but a stream. It was quiet, humble, unannounced– except for a small sign labeling it. I stood there in astonishment. This little river is the same one that carves the immense depth and grandeur of the Grand Canyon. Incredible! It all begins with ice melt from the

Rocky Mountains. This took me back to my parallels I had made while in Canyonlands about how in our lives there can be canyons, dark areas of sin that can be corrosive. I had previously concluded that canyons sometimes are formed by something so small and seemingly insignificant and sometimes in our lives it is those small things which over time gain power and eat away to corrupt a person. Here this was super evident. This dainty little stream, meandering so carefree through the sunny meadow, would become extremely powerful and corrosive, tearing away the land, creating profound depths and forming one of the greatest natural wonders of the world. This realization was a lot to take in.

I continued on my drive up Highway 34, Trail Ridge Road, through the pine forest. The drive took me over the Continental Divide and into altitudes well into the 11,000s

The Colorado River

which turned the landscape into alpine tundra. Here no trees nor shrubbery grew. The ground was either blanketed with short grass or covered in snow. I was up amongst mountain peaks, looking down into massive pine forests and valleys.

As I gained higher altitude, the road became something of a challenge, because it narrowed and hugged nothing. From the edge of the road dropped dramatic distances down into valleys. On top of it was a busy passage, with cars in sight in front of me, cars lined up behind me, and cars passing by very closely on my left. I needed complete focus. I was uneasy, clenching my steering wheel tightly. This road just didn't seem by any means safe. However I had no regrets. This was part of the adventure.

The climax to the drive was arriving at the Alpine Visitor Center. It was a break, a place to breathe at ease. It was also very busy. I drove around the parking lot several times before I found an open space. On one side of the parking lot was a snow-bank reaching well over twenty feet tall. Snow also blinded half of the windows at the visitor center. Getting outside my car, I noticed everything was kind of wet and dripping. It was a bright sunny June day, and temperatures had to be in the sixties. It was surprising to see that such an enormous snow bank still remained. It was telling of what the snowfall must have been like here in the winter.

From the parking lot I walked up a short trail to a mountain summit where many tourist stood around in shorts, taking photos of themselves and the great distances around them. I could feel the altitude. Breathing up here was not as effortless as it typically is in the world below. I then went into the visitor center adjoined by a large gift shop and cafeteria. I checked things out briefly and then walked across the road to the Ute Trail, where I began my first planned hike running. It was a great feeling to be running on top of a mountain, but snow was becoming deeper, slowing me down. Also the temperature was dropping out on the frozen expanse. I then realized how long this would take me with all the snow and how easily I could lose the trail. Reevaluating the situation, I decided it was a little too ambitious for the moment. I returned to the Alpine Visitor Center where I found a Rocky Mountain National Park t-shirt tie-dyed in the design of the Colorado flag. I bought it along with a hat and a book about the first 100 years of the National Park Service. Then it was off to find my campsite.

On the drive up in the alpine tundra I saw lot of wildlife. There were mountain goats, elk, and many marmots. I had gotten off at one overlook where a half dozen marmots were crawling and flopping around. This was my first ever time seeing a marmot. Frankly, I didn't know what a marmot was but had just learned to identify one in the visitor center. To me they look like a cross between a beaver and a woodchuck. In the eastern United States we don't have marmots, and it's not a very popular animal, thus its not built into our vocabulary. However, I love marmots. They are such goofy-looking animals with a cute charm about them and a high pitch short squeal that sounds like a smoke alarm when the battery needs to be changed. At this particular overlook, the marmots came very close to the

tourists, perhaps looking for handouts. It led way to me being able to get some great Marmot pictures, not only capturing the image of the animals, but the beautiful landscape in the background as well. I took one of the marmot stately posing on a rock with the most majestic valley and mountain view behind him. It was quite a photo.

I had descended the heights to Moraine Park Campground. My particular site, which I had reserved online, was one of my favorite campsites to date. From the car I had to walk a short distance to the edge of the forest where the trees led out into a prairie with a view of a mountain on the other side. The campsite was very private. I felt as if I had the whole prairie and mountain view to myself. I set up camp and, while doing so, made acquaintance with my neighboring campers. It was an elderly couple camping out of a small fancy looking retro camper connected to their vehicle by a hitch. They were from California and cleary had experience doing this. They were preparing dinner out of a kitchenette accessible from the outside on the back of their camper. I inquired if there were bear boxes or any food storage instructions I needed to be aware of. They assured me that bears wouldn't be a problem and nothing was out of the ordinary.

After camp was set up I drove a short distance to the small Bierstadt Lake. I took a peaceful walk around it on the trail loop. I observed a few men fly fishing, sporting their rubber waders and standing in water up to their waists. The late evening sky was clear and crisp and I admired the pristine reflection in deep rich colors of the mountains in the lake.

I felt a feeling of accomplished arrival. I knew I would be staying here for a few days, so I felt like I had fully checked in. I was successfully making my acquaintance and was at ease, knowing this would be a good stay in Rocky Mountain National Park.

I returned to my camp, to my secluded little hideout at the prairie's edge. I heated a can of soup and cooked oatmeal over the fire, while writing a few postcards. I watched the moon and stars come out and enjoyed the heat and crackle of my campfire next to me. I then retired to my tent where I had a relaxing readathon, reading over the park newspaper, another chapter in my book about the West, and the intro to my new history book about the National Park Service. All during this my campfire continued to subtly crack and send flickering warm glows across the side of my tent. This was a quintessential end of a day and included what I love most about camping– the beauty, the quiet, the simple comfort of nature, and the prospect of adventure in the day to come.

Bierstadt Lake

Trekking to Sky Pond

I was at the trailhead by 6am. I wanted to make sure I could squeeze in as much adventure as I could in this day and also make sure I could find parking. I hadn't yet put myself together so, within my car in the parking lot, I was changing out of my nighttime attire into layers for today's hike. I strapped up my boots, filled up my hydration pack, gathered my essential snacks, and fired up my hiking GPS. The destination was Sky Pond. According to the map it was a 9.8 mile hike nicely broken up into segments with Alberta Falls, Timberline Falls, Glass Lake, and Loch Lake all being points of interest along the way.

Unlike the hikes in Capitol Reef, where despite beauty and intrigue the miles stretched on forever, here the miles seem to pass by so quickly. It helped that I was full of energy and excitement, running nearly half of the distance. The weather was also amiable. The sky was perfectly rich blue, and the morning sun was bright but not painful. It shown enough to provide a warm touch on my face and arms, but in the shade the air was cool and brisk. It was an ideal balance making it prime hiking time. Surely all of nature's different attractions and vistas along the way made the hike so enjoyable that it passed by quickly. Also, I had stopped to take a plethora of photos, and today's views were the stuff of magazine quintessential perfection.

The first stopping point on the hike was Alberta Falls. It was a series of energetic cascades. The water rushed down in a white fury, leaping into a rapid stream around boulders adorned with lichen. Short pines stood along the rocky borders of the river. Their green complementary contrasted with the white rapids and the bright blue of the morning sky.

As the trail gradually ascended, it reached a point where I could see the Rocky Mountain giants through the tops of the pines. Their snowcapped heights looked so majestic. I soon came to the first lake—The Loch. The view was that of perfection. Bold rocky tops swooped down and reached tall as they surrounded the lake. In crevices all around, snow slid down the mountain heights. At the lower levels thin pines congregated quietly and uniformly. And then at the very bottom of view the cold dark lake water lay with tiny little ripple-like waves from the gentle breeze.

It was a very serene place. Except for one other hiker, a middle-aged man, I was alone. I faced the lake, closed my eyes, and took in a deep breath of the cold refreshing mountain air. Although often times I look for symbols in

Alberta Falls

the landscape around me and the voice of God to meet me out in the quietude of the wild, other times, like this one, I'm just filled of thankfulness. I am speechless, and in my mind I just keep saying "Thank you, God." I celebrate who God is, one who shares his beautiful creativity with us. Physical beauty and the pinnacle of artistic expression is found in wild natural places like this.

As I had paused here to take in the beauty the sun reached higher in the sky and positioned itself in such a way to permit the mountainscape to reflect perfectly the lake. After my rejuvenating and invigorating pause, I continued on my hike to Sky Pond.

As I was reaching higher altitude the landscape became covered in snow, and no thin layer of snow by any means, but feet of snow. Most of it was well compacted and icy, making it easy to stay on-top. I also took on the strategy of placing my feet in the footprints of hikers who had traveled on this days prior. Their footprints had turned into icy pads I could ground my feet on.

For a significant portion of trekking over snow the land was level and tame, and then I looked up to see a large incline completely covered in snow. To one side was a steep rock wall– to the other a jungle of rocks and Timberline Falls. The way up had to be between the two. The ground became steeper and the snow harder and icier. The only hint of a path was the footprints of others solidified in the snowmelt. The path curved around between the rock wall and the waterfall. The incline caused me to hunch over, leveraging my weight and using my hands on the ground for

Loch Lake

balance. I wasn't just following footprints. I was carefully placing my feet into small icy steps created by the trod of those who came before.

My heart began to race in nervousness. I was alone. I didn't know if this hike was supposed to be accomplished in such conditions. I didn't trust the terrain, and I didn't want to end up in my National Parks Search and Rescue book. If snow and ice had slipped out from under me, or I had lost my footing I would have gone tumbling and sliding down on the icy incline, and I wouldn't have slid exactly the way I came up. I wouldn't have slid down at such a curve. Instead I would have slid straight down in the jumble of rocks and into Timberline Falls. It would not have been good. I would have ended up in the book for sure. Times like these though, call for the trekking pole. Thank goodness I had saved it from the depths of Bryce Canyon. It came in handy here as an anchor to hold onto.

Eventually the icy footprints I had been following diminished. They led me right into the upper portion of Timberline Falls. Hmm, am I supposed to climb up the waterfall? I thought. I observed my surroundings. There was absolutely no other way. I didn't come all this way to give up now, I thought. Onward I must go!

There were parts of the cascade I would not set foot on, like the parts almost entirely covered in snow where I could hear the rush of water but could not see it. However, the section I was taking on was the exposed and clearly frozen part of the falls, where icy rocks were jumbled together, and the collection of rocks was enough and varied that there

were places to put my feet and grab on to hoist myself up. I had worked up a sweat on this journey, and the sun was getting warmer, so here I was maneuvering through a frozen cascade in a tank top but my hands were cold. I wanted gloves.

There were a couple movements I needed to make to hoist myself up rocks in which I had to stop myself from letting panic set in. Instead I relied on my animal instincts of survival. I would climb up this cascade! I would see Sky Pond!

And I did! It was amazing. It was similar to the Loch, but at this altitude fewer trees remained, and snow and ice melt reflected so artistically on the lake. I climbed up a large nearby rock. From here I stood and looked behind at the beautiful valley I had traversed to get to this point. I could see the pine forests squeezed in between rock giants, one of the lakes already passed, and the other mountains in the distance. Up here the beauty was so transcending, the air so brisk, but the sun so warming. It was all so relaxing. It put me at ease. I decided to place my backpack down as a pillow, put on my light hoodie, and lay down hugging myself and deeply breathing the rich mountain air. I didn't think it was possible here but I fell asleep for a good twenty minutes. I awoke to greet the beautiful view with a renewed lens. I don't ever recall waking up to a sight so beautiful in my life. This was pure bliss. I sat there, quietly taking it all in.

Other hikers had arrived. It was a family— mom, dad, brother, sister, and grandma. I had my moment and I decided I would venture back down on the trail, but I didn't want to descend the icy cascade and the slick snowscape. There must be another way I thought. And so I started down the other side of Timberline Falls. After climbing and scrambling down immensities of rock my efforts proved fruitless. I wouldn't be able to get down successfully. The terrain became impossible so I backtracked up to Sky Pond, and by this time the family who had also been enjoying the lake had begun their descent. *Perfect,* I thought. *I will follow them and see how its done.* They carefully and successfully climbed down the waterfall and then, on their behinds, they went sliding down the snowscape. I was the caboose trailing grandma, and I'm glad I was, because I thought to myself, *If grandma can do this, then certainly I can.* And P.S. What a lady! Grandma and I got into a bit of small talk until I squatted down and slid on my boots back to level ground. The family was very pleasant and clearly adventurous. On the way back we all helped each other out finding the best routes over the snow and through the woods. At this time of day other hikers had embarked on this same adventure. We gave warnings of the challenges ahead as they inquired.

Eventually, about halfway in the return, I arrived back at the junction with the path that leads to Jewels Lake. I decided to take the side trip and check out Jewels Lake. It was a crowded area with a smaller, but nevertheless beautiful lake. Many tourists were taking photos of themselves and each other. I was clearly not the only hiker in a tank top and shorts. Later I would find a photo of my mom's dad, Grandpa Wolf, in the same location.

Grandpa Wolf

When I got back to my car I checked my GPS. My 9.8 mile hike had turned into around 14 miles. I added that to my hiking miles tally and was glad to bump my miles hiked up significantly. I was surprised at all the miles hiked because it was still only early afternoon.

Immediately I was able to determine this was my favorite hike to date. The amazing views, matched with the snowy challenges, and traversing a waterfall just made it so unique and such an experience. To me, one of the factors that makes a good hike are the challenges it presents, whether climbing up a waterfall, descending by rope, crossing riverbeds, or scrambling up rock faces. It's the challenges that add a sense of accomplishment and create stories to be shared.

The rest of my day was largely uneventful. I had driven into Estes Park which was very crowded, touristy, and distasteful for my liking. The only thing I left Estes Park with was a Subway sandwich. I returned to the National Park and sought out a picnic area to enjoy my sandwich. I ended up just eating it in a parking lot at one of the overlooks in the alpine tundra, because the view was exceptionally breathtaking this time of day. A large capstone like cluster of clouds had congregated to cover the sun and darken the sky, but a break in the clouds allowed for light beams to shoot down and illuminate the snowy mountains.

I hadn't thought about it in the moment, but now as I observe and reflect over the photographs, I draw parallels to the light beams shining down and illuminating the dark canyons in Canyonlands National Park. I wonder if, in this moment, God was speaking to me, telling me He will take those canyons and turn them into mountains, taking the deep dark broken places of life and building them up to strong unwavering peaks.

Finding my way out of these canyons in life could be like this day's hikes— a journey met with challenges, but the challenges not setbacks, and the challenges not hindering but rather spurring me on to overcome. As I embark on a quest to traverse and confront my canyons, I will approach them with the attitude of today's hike: I didn't come all this way to give up now. And when it's complete and my canyons are raised to mountains, I will reflect and gaze upon the new beauty, feeling the accomplishment and wonder. Greatest of all, I will have a new story to tell of the power and beauty of God.

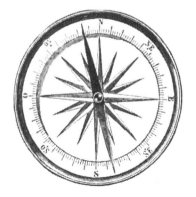

LOST ON MOUNT IDA

"You'll never make it," she warned, returning to the parking lot from her intended hike. Never make it? *Do you know who you are talking to? This is Josh Hodge, the one who has found his way out after falling into Bryce Canyon, the one who yesterday climbed a frozen cascade to Sky Pond. I will make it,* I said in my mind. The goal was to hike to the top of Mount Ida, via the Continental Divide over the alpine tundra. I had seen pictures. It looked stunning. "The snow is too deep. You'll lose the trail," she continued.

I could have taken her warning to heart, but without a doubt I knew I had to try for myself. I've lived enough life to know I can't always trust what people say. I mean, after all, people were saying the world would end with Y2K, Donald Trump would never become president, and Anakin Skywalker would bring balance to the force, yet here we are. And now try and tell me it's impossible to summit Mount

Ida. We'll just see about that.

So I proceeded all geared up, and only after a few
yards in I began asking myself, *now wait a minute…where is the
trail?* Snow completely covered everything, and here I was
basically at the beginning of the hike, questioning where the
trail was. I could only see in retrospect that this would be
foreshadowing of the entire experience. It was good that to
begin with there were footprints to follow. Some hikers had
taken a switchback approach while others made steep
shortcuts. Not knowing which was the proper route I ended
up taking a little of both routes. The trail had left the small
parking lot and ascended into the pine forest, and that is
when the footprints disappeared. The snow was now up to
my knees. Every once in a while I would sink down into the
snow, but at other times my feet remained on top the frozen snowpack.

If I were a trail which way would I go? That became my
train of thought. Following a switchback approach no
longer seemed feasible, because the incline was too steep
and there was no seemingly possible way to hike alongside
the mountain. Only going vertical seemed possible. And so
I proceeded, only soon to find out that it might be a little
too steep. If my feet would slip and lose grip of the snow I
would plummet down this mountainside, crashing back into
the parking lot and maybe banging my head against rocks
on the way down. I cautiously maneuvered my way up to a
small patch of level ground. To the right there was more
incline. In front of me there was even more, and to the left
there were rocks and the sound of water rushing under the

snow. Since I could hear water but not see it, it made me begin to question what other things were hidden under the snow. What sort of crevices, ravines, water sources and perils were hidden from sight? I treaded toward the rush of water, slowly, carefully placing my steps trying to assure myself the ground was stable under the snow. This was too much. *This can't be the way up,* I thought. I had to have missed something. I concluded I needed to backtrack. The only problem was going down I had ascended was very intimidating.

My feet were able to grip their way up but would obviously slide on their way down. I scanned the scene to feed it into my problem solving matrix. Here was the plan: *If I fall, I fall, but I need to strategically plan my fall so that I can stop myself by clinging onto, or falling into, trees along the way.*

3-2-1 go!

I slid, falling down on my behind. And Thump! I hit tree one…and thump! tree two. Phew! I made it to the level ground. My heart was racing, but a smile spread across my face. That was pretty fun. I was the ball traveling down the pinball machine.

From another place of level ground I made a decision to attempt the switchback method, so I snuggled up against the mountain and slowly shimmied my way against it. I was ascending, slowly but surely, leaving the bald landscape and returning back into the forest. The snow became increasingly deeper. I found myself trudging through snow up to my waist. I came to realize this was no switchback route because there were no turns in direction of incline. My route was all in the same direction. I also came to realize the snow depth had grown much deeper than my waist. My weight sunk into the snow in such a way that the depth was measured by my waist but my feet were still standing on a great measure of compacted snow. This could be ten or twenty feet deep, I began to realize. Each step became a moment of uneasiness. How far would I sink in? I feared sinking so deep that I would be stuck. I tried clinging onto the grey rock face to my left, but every so often I would lose grip and sink into the snow.

I was completely alone again. No one else had taken this route or made it this far. The parking lot was now far behind and below me. Everyone else had given up much sooner. *I should have too,* I thought. The prospect of falling deep into the snow, being stuck, and never having anyone find me was horrifying. I had to get out of here. I could see dirt and rock up ahead. I was presently just on top and in the middle of a giant snow drift.

When I reached ground again I gave off a sigh of relief. It was like I had just been walking on top of clouds, knowing their density was not consistent, knowing I could fall through at any moment. What a relief it was to be on solid ground. I could stomp ground firmly under my boots. My legs felt wobbly and disoriented, sort of the feeling I get after swimming or riding a bicycle for an extended period of time. I looked ahead through the trees and there was a bald— a section of tundra free from snow jutting off the side of the mountain. I proceeded to it knowing here I could get a glimpse of the environment surrounding me and assess the situation.

I caught something colorful with my eyes. Resting against a tree on the edge of the bald was a small canister. This was exciting in two ways. First off, it was a sign that I wasn't the only human to take this route. Someone else, at some point, had made it up here so perhaps there was an easier way down. Secondly, it's a geocache! I thought. Geocaching is an outdoor activity where one follows GPS coordinates to find hidden objects. Oftentimes they are small canisters containing little trinkets and a log book to sign off on your accomplishment. I had just begun geocaching in the spring and had even done a bit with my parents at the beginning of the summer. How cool to accidentally stumble upon a geocache, I thought.

I raced over to the canister. It was made of pottery and painted all over in bright colors. How fancy, I observed. I opened it and to my dismay it contained nothing but dirt. Befuddled, I put the lid back on it and examined the container. Among the colorful design were the white letters "Noah" painted. Under the name were two dates, the latter 1997, revealing to me that these were the ashes of a teenager named Noah. Feeling a bit uncomfortable, like I had just desecrated something sacred, I set the canister down. *Have his ashes been up here since 1997? No way! Are those ashes inside or just dirt?* I didn't want to think about it. I proceeded to the bald and took a few pictures. The mountainous landscape around me, suggested nothing about what my next move should be. I knew I did not want to attempt continuing up the mountain, but I did not want to attempt going back the way I came, and I had no idea in what direction my next move should be. I returned and sat down next to Noah. "Well…" I told him, "we are lost together," but the stark contract was that I was alive and he wasn't. It's like in a movie when someone gets locked in a creepy dungeon cell, or stuck in a remote cave, and a skeleton sits there as a warning that no one makes it out alive. That's the type of feeling I entertained for a moment. However, I knew Noah didn't die here. He was placed.

Then…*What's that sound?* No, it wasn't Noah. There were other hikers coming from another direction. "Over here" I called out. I came upon a pair of hikers, also lost. They were two guys, maybe ten years older than myself, who had come up a different route but were now lost. They inquired about how I came up. I pointed but told them I didn't suggest it. One of them went over to observe my route and turned around. "I told you so." We decided to divide and conquer in attempt to find a route. We split up, each going in a different direction. None of us were successful and rejoined in the middle. "How about that way?" One guy pointed in an unpromising direction. I followed. I didn't necessarily trust that these guys would bring us back to the parking lot, but I thought it's better to be lost with other people, other alive people that is, than just with Noah.

We started descending into a valley on a very shallow covering of snow. While doing so we got to talking about hiking and national parks and onto the topic of Yosemite and the hike I have not yet done up to the top of Half Dome. On our journey we came to a barren area with lumps of wispy grass frozen and covered over with snow.

Here we came upon another hiker. He became the leader of the pack, assuring us a way back to the parking lot. We all proceeded as a ragtag pack of hikers, who all got lost, who all got defeated by Mount Ida, but who were so appreciative of finding each other.

I sat back down in my car, relieved to no longer be lost, feeling the humbling effect of defeat and replaying the words of the sassy girl, "you'll never make it." She was right. I failed. However, what a story! Getting lost, finding Noah, teaming up as a pack of hikers to find our way out. It was a good experience. I was satisfied. Sometimes I feel like I have the instinct to prove others wrong, and sometimes those instances of attempted proof are not always successful but are instead met with failure. But it's in failure that I learn humility, I discover my limits, and come away with stories to tell. So, tell me again I can't do something. Watch me succeed or watch me fail. Either way I come out better off.

Chillin' Like a Moose

"Why, hello there," I said to the moose who chose to make my acquaintance. He nonchalantly came by as if we were old friends. I sat at a picnic table off to the side of Coyote Valley. I heard a rustle in the brush behind me and a moose emerged ever so unfazed.

I had read some notices about moose, how they can be dangerous, how they can charge. This moose didn't seem the least bit aggressive. He was just out for a mid-day stroll, enjoying the park just like all the other visitors. I reached for my camera to take his picture but the lighting just wasn't enough. The pictures weren't very satisfying. I put the camera away and took in this moment of an up close encounter with a moose.

I had been sitting there, relaxing, enjoying the beautiful view of the valley and writing in my journal reflections on my experience in Canyonlands. I was writing about my emotional experience sitting on the canyon rim and the voice of

God speaking to me ever so clearly. Tears of thankfulness and spiritual renewal fell down upon the pages. Then the moose arrived, and that particular emotional moment ended as I was faced with another of excitement. I had seen photographers with huge lenses trying to take photos of wildlife elsewhere in this park and other parks, but here I was just feet away from a giant moose walking slowly and carefree. I was putting forth no effort in being able to see the moose. It just strolled right past me. Sometimes the greatest things just come so unexpectantly and nonchalantly.

After the moose passed by I felt my visit to Coyote Valley had been fulfilled. I had finished writing the entry in my journal and was ready to move on and see what Grand Lake was all about.

This morning I had attempted but failed to reach the top of Mount Ida. That was followed by a stop at the Alpine Visitor Center where I had lunch in the cafeteria. I then had proceeded to Holzwarth Historic District. There a short trail leads through the meadow of the valley to the guest cabins from an old ranch of the early 1900s which is now preserved by the National Park Service. The cabins are furnished like they would have been back in the day. I couldn't go inside but I peeked in all the windows and imagined what it would have been like to stay here years ago. This all led up to me finding my way to Coyote Valley where I had stopped to write and met the moose.

Now I was on my way to Grand Lake. Grand Lake is the name of the lake and town on the southwest side of the park. I had camped next to the lake on my second night of visiting the Rockies. Although the lake was beautiful to see at night, my campsite was right next to a road, and my neighbors seemingly enjoyed top forty hits instead of the sound and solitude of nature. That night I had left my campsite to sit in my car by the lake. There I brushed my teeth and enjoyed the beauty of the scene. I had collected enough water gallons that by now I had figured out a system of brushing my teeth in my car. This sticks in my memory, because it was the most beautiful place I ever brushed my teeth. The lake, the mountains, the stars, the cool night sky— it was all so nice, and this is where I also first implemented my non bathroom brushing teeth procedures which would come in handy later in campgrounds without running water.

Holzwarth Ranch

Grand Lake

The next morning I packed the tent first thing. Although I had reserved and paid to stay here another night, I just couldn't bear to wake up to Katy Perry roaring again. From here I had traveled into the park. I arrived by 7 a.m. and was able to secure a site inside the park at Timber Creek. When I was setting up camp an elk walked right through the campsite next to mine and paused, just chillin' like the moose.

While setting up my tent, I couldn't find the tent fly. I had concluded I must have left it at the campground by Grand Lake. I drove all the way back to check. I didn't see it nor had my pop-infused neighbors. Come to find out, I set my tent up in Timber Creek right on top the fly. This all happened in the morning, and by evening here I was returning to Grand Lake once again. I wanted to check out the

Grand Lake Lodge and have dinner downtown.

As I approached the driveway to Grand Lake Lodge I wasn't sure if it was acceptable for one such as I, lowly and penny pinching to visit such a wealthy establishment. And I didn't know just how fancy the place was. I didn't know if there would be some sort of snazzy valet parking. I didn't know if I could freely walk into the lobby, but I thought hey, why not find out? Plus it's a lodge. Just the term evokes a sort of friendliness.

I had walked into the lodge at Bryce Canyon and had hung out quite a bit in their lobby, but the difference here was that this lodge was not technically in the National Park. It was right outside the park. I arrived and decided I would play it like I was a guest staying there. So I walked right in the lobby and out the backdoor where the patio and pool were. It was a stunning view with the pool right next to the

beautiful lake with Rocky Mountains surrounding it. It was-
n't a very big pool but it was quite busy. I noticed signs for a
wedding.

I went inside and browsed the gift shop. The lobby
was made of all wood and was nice, but there was nothing
too extraordinary about it. The view of the lake out the back
was what made this place well worth the stop. Inside I decided to take a break and sit for a while on a swinging bench
and free some memory on my camera card.

After resting at Grand Lake Lodge I proceeded into
Grand Lake. There I at dinner at a place called Sagebrush
which I had read about on TripAdvisor. The food was delicious and the helping was heaping, even for the ravenous
hiker I was. I had a BBQ half chicken, mashed potatoes,
baked beans, and cornbread. The waitress was very friendly.

She asked me many questions. "Are you traveling alone? Where are you from? Where are you camping?" She told me that she thought I was extremely "cool" and that she would love to be doing what I was doing. She gave me a recommendation on a free place to camp, but I didn't know where she was referring to. She was very attentive and came over to talk to me frequently. I am not good at picking up signals but this was very evident. She wanted to make a connection, but I could not connect with her like the young lady at the Petrified Forest.

After my meal, I walked along the main street in my flip flops. I let my feet breathe, and I just walked slowly and carefree– at ease, just like the moose, with no hurry. I looked in the shop windows and passed by many restaurants. It was touristy, but with a more tactful and homey feel than its rival, Estes Park, which was overly crowded and blaringly commercial for my liking.

Along my walk I stopped for some cherry chocolate chip ice cream and walked over to a park which was more like a city green. I noticed a gazebo in the middle and this reminded me of something. Presently, and for the past few days, I was in a power crisis. My cell phone battery had died, and I couldn't charge it in the car because I had blown a fuse. I didn't know at the time that it was just an easy fix fuse issue. I thought the charging outlet was broken entirely. However, I had no way to charge my phone in the car. I had drained the battery from my Chromebook into my phone, yet the phone was still soon to lose power. I had been on a lookout for outlets. Unfortunately no bathrooms in the National Park had outlets. Two days prior, when passing through a small town nearby, there was a local visitor center where there was a private bathroom with an outlet. I took my time in that bathroom in order to try and pick up some charge for my phone.

Here, now in Grand Lake, I had noticed outlets inside the park gazebo. Perfect! I grabbed my chargers in my car and plugged in my devices in the gazebo. There was a pair of young teenage lovers there as well, which didn't even make things awkward. I didn't care. I had important priorities. I needed power. There was also Wi-Fi. It was important for me to keep my phone on because I was waiting for a call or text from my cousin Jonathan. There was talk of meeting up with him and some other family within the next few days. I was anxiously awaiting communication from him. It would determine my route of travel, and I didn't want to miss the opportunity to connect.

After sitting in the park gazebo for a while, uploading some photos to the internet, and finishing my ice cream, I headed back into the National Park, back to my campsite for my final night in the Rocky Mountains. It had been a hodgepodge of a day, from packing up and setting up camp in the early a.m. with an elk by my side, to getting lost on route to Mount Ida and encountering Noah, making my way to the Holzwarth cabins and Coyote Valley where I met a moose, visiting Grand Lake Lodge, and then taking in downtown with delicious food. Tomorrow the adventure would continue, looping around Colorado, heading down to Great Sand Dunes National Park and Preserve, and reconnecting with my cousins.

Grandpa Hodge

Somewhere between Rocky Mountain National Park and Great Sand Dunes National Park and Preserve, before I could call my dad and wish him a Happy Father's Day, my cell phone rang. My parents broke the news to me that my Grandpa Hodge had passed away this morning in his sleep.

I pulled over to a gas station and spoke with my parents and let the news sink in. Grandpa Hodge would be missed, but we were also fully aware this day was coming. Grandpa had been in and out of the hospital many times. We had seen him suffer in a state of deteriorated health and immobility.

Grandpa Hodge was many things to many people. He loved his wife, his family, and bringing everyone together. He was friendly to others, generous to his family, full of stories and experiences, and too held a spirit of adventure. Never living near my grandparents, I usually saw my grandparents on special occasions during our summer trips to Illinois or when he and Grandma came out to visit us on vacation in Massachusetts.

I wanted to make it to the funeral but it wouldn't be feasible from my location. Later this day, when I was able to connect to the internet, I posted this statement along with his photo which was shared at his funeral:

"Today we say goodbye to Grandpa Hodge. What a man! He was a real family man who cherished his life and family. Here I am out exploring the wonders of our great nation, thinking of how my Grandpa too was a man of travel, but for the past many years he hasn't been able to travel and see new things because of illness and immobility. I was hit with some powerful emotion today imagining my Grandpa in Heaven, mobile, full or energy, restored to his true self, and being able to explore new places far more beautiful than anything this world has to offer. Grandpa will be missed, but he's finished the race, and I'm proud of him."

On June 20th the Bureau County Republican published this obituary:

"PRINCETON — Raymond H. Hodge, 87, of Princeton passed away peacefully at home in his sleep on Father's Day morning, June 19, 2016. He was a cherished husband as well as a beloved father to five children, 13 grandchildren and seven great-grandchildren.

Born Aug. 11, 1928, in Ewing to Raymond F. and Jewell M. (Martin) Hodge, he married Betty J. Warling Dec. 26, 1951, in Princeton. She survives.

He moved with his parents from southern Illinois to the Manlius-New Bedford area around 1948. He served two years in the Army during the Korean War. Upon returning from Korea, he got a job stocking shelves at the Piggly Wiggly grocery store near the fairgrounds in Princeton. Within four years, he was promoted to manager and remained the manager for 30 years in which time Piggly Wiggly became the Eagle Super Market, occupying the building that is now the Princeton Public Library. Retiring at the age of 59, he spent his retirement years enjoying vacations with his wife, his children and grandchildren. He also enjoyed visiting presidential homes and sitting on his front porch in the summertime saying "hello there" to passersby, an activity he enjoyed on his last night in this life.

Before ill health struck, he attended the First Christian Church in Princeton for many years, as well as the Hampshire Colony Church.

Survivors include his five children...13 grandchildren...seven great-grandchildren.. one brother...and two sisters

He was preceded in death by his parents, two sisters and one brother.

Funeral services will be at 10:30 a.m. Thursday, June 23, at the Norberg Memorial Home in Princeton with the Rev. Michael Hodge officiating. Burial will be in Elm Lawn Memorial Park in Princeton…"

Me and Grandpa Hodge

On the Great Sand Dunes

I could see them from seventy miles away, the Great Sand Dunes of Colorado. I was intrigued by this park well before arriving. It was another park I heard very little about. It was founded as a National Monument in 1932 by Herbert Hoover but gained the title National Park and Preserve in 2004 by an act of Congress. Sand dunes have always fascinated me just because they are so different than anything I'm used to. This would be my fourth trip to desert sand dunes. The first was my harrowing plight for survival in a sand storm in Death Valley. The second was in Coral Pink Sand Dunes State Park in southern Utah, where I peacefully watched the sunset over the pink sand. My third experience was in Huacachina, Peru where I went sand-boarding with my brother Nathan and sister-in-law Catherine.

I had driven about five hours from Rocky Mountain National Park to Great Sand Dunes National Park and Preserve. It was now the middle of the day.

While I was approaching the park, I was again draining my battery from my Chromebook into my cell phone. I had tried plugging the charging cord from my phone directly into the USB port in the car. I thought it was charging, but all along it was wasting battery. I had on and off communication with my cousin, Jonathan, days prior. I knew he and other family were in Colorado, but I didn't know their exact whereabouts nor plans. I was trying to connect with them. I assumed draining a Chromebook battery into a cell phone was not good for the life of the Chromebook battery, but I remembered the purpose of buying this Chromebook in the first place. I had purchased it super cheap the summer before just outside of McFarland, California simply to back up photos from my travels. This device was meant to be an emergency travel device, and connecting with my cousins and aunt would be far more valuable than this piece of technology. Arriving at Great Sand Dunes National Park and Preserve I still had no plans with my cousins. I didn't know why reaching them was so difficult, but later I would learn why.

Great Sand Dunes National Park and Preserve is a very isolated park. I drove many miles in wide open space with very little civilization in sight. I had spoken to a Park Ranger about this park the following summer in Grand Teton National Park. He told me that this park was petitioned to transition from a National Monument to a National Park in efforts to increase tourism in the area.

When I arrived at the park my first stop was the

campground. Plan A was to set up camp in the park campground. Plan B was to obtain a wilderness permit and camp out in the sand dunes. I was able to pursue Plan A, as there were still a few sites left. I thought arriving mid-day I would have no luck, but perhaps because this place was so very hot, maybe it wasn't quite appealing for the general camper.

The campsite I chose faced the sand dunes but I could only see one large dune which served as a wall, hiding all the curves and waves of the other dunes behind it

I quickly set up Kelty, hopped in my car, and drove to the visitor center. Then I was off to the dunes. There are no trails on the dunes. There is simply a large parking lot and the great sand expanse. I applied sunscreen in plenty, filled up my hydration pack, and then needed to make a decision about footwear. I thought I had come up with a brilliant idea. I didn't want to wear my boots because I thought they would be too heavy in the sand. I didn't want to wear my tennis shoes because I knew they would collect sand, especially since one of my shoes had caught on fire from campfire embers and had a nice hole burnt through the top. I was imagining the sand collecting in my shoes and making the trek uncomfortable. I knew I couldn't go barefoot, because there were many warning signs about that. The park warned that in the summer afternoon the sand can reach temperatures up to 150 degrees. My genius idea was to go in socks.

A group of young adventurers from a vehicle next to me approached "Do you know what we should wear out there," one of them asked as I was getting myself together.

"I am just going like this,' I replied, standing shirtless in a pair of blue gym shorts and socks.

"Have you been here before?"

"No I haven't" I replied

"What should we wear on our feet?"

"I don't know, but I'm just wearing socks."

"That's a good idea," he replied. I thought so to. I was glad to share my wisdom.

I began my trek barefoot because at first there was a stretch of water trickling down from snow melt in the mountains far away creating a very shallow river on top the sand. Many people were congregated in this area. Children ran about splashing in the water and playing with the sand as if at the beach.

After crossing the water the incline began, and the expanse of dry hot desert dunes stretched on for miles. Socks were on and traveling was great. Although the area of sand dunes was very expansive, it was not endless. In all directions were the tall rocky mountains of Colorado with pine trees and snow melt creating stripes down their sides. It was an interesting contrast to be in stifling hot sand dunes looking around at mountains with snow. It was also interesting to think that just yesterday I was venturing through deep snow drifts on my attempt to make it to Mount Ida. Colorado is definitely a place of contrasts.

The sand dunes were relatively busy. People were following each other's footprints to dune peaks. As typical, I wanted to to go farther than everyone else. So I trudged further and further up and down sand dunes, which is not easy. It takes maybe five times the effort than hiking on solid ground, because with each step your feet sink, and there is not stable ground to push yourself off of. Hiking downward is fun though, because you can descend inclines too steep and perilous for solid ground. On sand there's no harm done when you fall, tumble, and slide. The sand is a giant encompassing cushion.

Here the color of the sand was uniformly a typical beige color. No plants grew. It was everything you might imagine sand dunes to be. Nothing out of the ordinary like pink sand, or black sand, or wild scary-looking desert shrubs. It was just a giant sand box of a place.

I had reached the highest dune I could see from when I began my quest. Standing on top, I could see there were more mighty dunes in the distance, which were tempting to pursue. But at the moment, my feet felt like they were on fire. Wearing socks was not a bright idea. Hot sand found its way into the socks over and over again, and was burning my feet. The hot sand mixed with coarse friction had also burned and ripped a giant hole in one of my socks. It appeared as if part of the sock had disintegrated. I was about a mile and a half in, but my feet couldn't endure anymore hiking, so I turned around. I wasn't disappointed the least bit. I felt like I got a true Great Sand Dunes experience greater than the rest of the tourists who gave up much sooner than me.

On the way back I remember sitting down for a moment and looking around at the sand, the mountains, and the people way below. I remember thinking, *How in the world did I get here?* Although I knew the answer, it was all sort of a marvel to me that I found myself in such a unique and different place than where I typically live my life. This sort of moment had happened more than once on my trip. In these pauses I try to take it all in. My life sort of replays through my mind. It's a summary of my weaknesses that I conjure up. I think back to when I was a teenager, being so depressed that I didn't care to be alive anymore. At that time self-doubt and insecurity ripped me apart inside, and my world was so small. It didn't extend beyond my own feelings. I also think back to college when I was incredibly sick and weak, plagued with complicated Ulcerative Colitis and Pancreatitis. I grew tired climbing just one flight of stairs. Then I was hospitalized. I remember when I was able to walk again. I went out into the hospital courtyard with my walker, and just being able to stand on my feet, clinging onto my walker in that little landscape patch between cement buildings, was enough for me to find hope.

Now, here I was sitting on top of a giant sand dune in the beating sun, thousands of miles removed from home, alive, strong, and full of spirit. I'd come from the Sonoran Desert, seeing Saguaro cactus, through the Petrified Forest, across the plains of the Navajo Nation, around the canyons of Utah, up to aspen forests and alpine tundra of Colorado, and now here I was on a giant sand dune. I'd climbed higher than everyone else. They tired before me. I looked down at them as little ants. I realized my past was marked by canyons of illness that kept me trapped in low places, but now I was on a mountain, not by my own doing, but by the force of restoration and strength attributed to God.

In addition to marveling at how far I'd come, I was also struck in wonder by the diverse beauty of the United States. A few years ago I would have never even imagined that such a place as Great Sand Dunes National Park and Preserve existed in the United States. The more and more I travel to National Parks, the more I fall in love with this country. It is so full and rich in natural beauty. I remember when I was younger I thought the United States was just sort of uniform place with varying degrees in temperature. I couldn't have been more wrong. The United States is amazingly rich in geological diversity. The National Park service does a great job at preserving all of these wonders and surprises.

After trying to take it all in I began my hike down the sand dunes back to my car, tumbling and sliding down, despite my feet being in much pain. I had to arch my feet, trying to keep contact with sand limited to the tips of my toes and my heels. I had to pause at times and raise one foot up in the air to give it a chance to cool off, cooling down from the 150 degrees of the sand to the 105 degrees of the air. It was such a relief when I got back to the shallow river and placed my feet in the ice melt water. I hoped the other young travelers from the parking lot hadn't followed my example in footwear.

I would have stayed longer in the river if it weren't for some intrusive ranchera music blaring and ruining the serenity. A group of people had set up a canopy by the river

where they had a picnic and enjoyed their choice music. I
would have been happy listening to the water trickle and
the wind wisp across the sand. It's okay. I let it go. I wanted to go relax at my campsite and figure out a plan for the
evening from there.

Back at my site I had received a text from my
cousin Jonathan. He and his family had been busy white
water rafting most of the day, but now they were done and
staying at an Airbnb in Durango, Colorado. I was welcomed to come spend the night, visit Mesa Verde the following day, and then backpack overnight in the San Juan
Mountains to the Ice Lakes the next day.

I plugged in the address into my GPS. They were
about 160 miles away, which would equal roughly three
hours of travel. I would arrive at night, but it wouldn't be a
problem. Sign me up!

I tore down my tent and threw it back into my car. I
found the campground host to inquire about a refund. She
said refunds are never issued but I could sell my campsite.
So I peddled around and sold my site to a couple at a
slightly discounted price. Then I was out of there.

Durango, here I come! I was excited to see family. I
had seen my cousin Jonathan the summer before when we
adventured around Yosemite National Park together. It
was a memorable time, and he was great company. That
was the last time I'd seen him. I would have liked to have
seen him more, but I lived in Kentucky and he was sta-
tioned in California with the Air Force. As kids we were
decently close, although I would only see him in the sum-

mer when my family would travel back to Princeton, Illinois. I thought we had a pretty good cousin bond, given our limited time together, but then the expanse of time grew larger between us and we grew up. When we met up in Yosemite it had been years since I'd spent any time with him. I wasn't sure how our interactions would go, but I couldn't have asked for a better adventure buddy and a better time. Sure, we had grown and time brought change, but we were family and we were able to reconnect effortlessly and have a great time.

I also hadn't seen my cousin Paul and his wife, Ines, in a few years. They had been living in Germany and their lives would be very different from what I last knew. And then there was my aunt Mary who lived in Illinois, whom I hadn't seen in even a longer period of time. I knew she had endured heavy challenges and changes in life, and I admired her for her strength and raising my cousins, whom I respect so greatly, in the midst of it. I was so excited to see all of them and go on adventures together.

When I arrived Cousin Paul and Aunt Mary were still awake. I spoke with them for a while, filling them in on my adventures and them filling me in on theirs. Their white water rafting trip was seriously legit. They rode some high class rapids and took the famous Durango and Silverton Railroad to their launching point. After visiting with them I got laundry started, took a much needed shower, shaved, and retired to the living-room floor where they all had kindly left the comforters from their beds. I had a plush island of comfiness to myself, luxurious compared to the weeks of tent camping I had grown used to.

I was happy. Although I hadn't seen these family members together in a long time, there was comfort in being with them. I had found a little piece of home way out in Colorado.

MESA VERDE WITH MY COUSINS

The living room floor was covered in gear and supplies all laid out and organized in piles and distinct sections. We were prepping for our overnight backpacking journey up into the San Juan Mountains to camp in a basin by the Ice Lakes. We had to divvy up supplies to see whose pack could carry which things. We hadn't even begun our journey, but I was excited. The spirit of adventure was alive and thriving.

I had never backpacked overnight with anyone and here we were, this was actually going to happen! And for once I didn't have to take the lead. My cousin Paul had sought this trail and plan. He had seen it online while in Germany and had been waiting to do it next time he was in the United States. I was relieved to be a follower. All I needed to do was make sure I packed what I needed for the ad-

venture. My Aunt Mary, Cousin Jonathan, Cousin Paul and
his wife Ines were all packing at the same time, asking each
other questions, trading off supplies, helping each other
come to decisions about what was best. I loaned Paul an in-
flatable pillow, and I volunteered to carry the majority of the
water supply. Jonathan volunteered his pack to carry our
bear canister with most of our food supply. We weren't sure
if there were even bears in the mountains, but better safe
than sorry. Food, however, wasn't our strongest of priorities, but we packed what would sustain us. We had apples,
peanut butter and jelly sandwiches, jerky, Clif bars, and trail
mix. I had also tucked away in my backpack some electrolyte gummies. I had noticed how useful they had been on
other hikes.

A couple of us had hiking backpacks, but some of
the others had standard back-to-school type backpacks
bulging with camp supplies. So we got creative, tying things
to packs with ropes and miscellaneous straps. We didn't
have the most deluxe backpacking gear, but we were going
to make this work.

When we finished packing I went out on the terrace
of the adobe-like apartment Airbnb we were staying in and
sat there with Paul and Ines. We were relaxing and snacking
on some vegetables and cherries, enjoying the summer heat
slowly fade in the late evening, and writing in the guest book
for the Airbnb. The host lived in an apartment on the bottom floor of the building. I didn't meet her, but the others
had been there for a couple days and apparently she had
been very friendly and had even brought homemade break-

fast bread to them. I was able to sample it. It was delicious.

Sometimes it's the simplest things that stick out more apparent in our memories. Sitting here on this terrace with my cousins is just such a fond memory of mine. Three things about it made it special to me. First off, it was the conclusion to such a fine day. We had spent the day touring around Mesa Verde National Park. It was also the eve of a grand adventure into the San Juan Mountains, and it was also the joy and comfort of reconnecting and resting in the company of family after having been alone for weeks.

In the morning we had arrived at Mesa Verde early, shortly after the park opened. We wanted to make sure we could secure tickets for a tour of the Cliff Palace. It was a success, and my Aunt Mary kindly purchased the tickets for all of us. I then made sure we all stopped to see the park film because, personally for me, we know a National Park visit is not complete without seeing the park film. After that we went on a short hike up to the top of the mesa where we took some nice cousinly photos and looked down at the winding road we had ascended in the park.

Our tour of the Grand Palace went well. The tour took us down around and inside the famous cliff dwellings that come to most minds when Mesa Verde is mentioned. The large and intricate rock house city hidden under the overhang of the mesa was impressive. There were about fifteen of us on the tour. We were guided and informed by a rather round Native American park ranger with a black braided ponytail sticking out behind his ranger hat. He carried with him a spray bottle, and along the tour he asked us tourists trivia questions. If any of us were correct we earned a spray from his bottle. It sounds silly, and I thought it was a little much at first, but the second time I answered a question correctly I gladly accepted a spray. The dry summer heat of southern Colorado is oppressive. Any relief should always be accepted.

What's most fascinating to me about Mesa Verde is how the inhabitants of this place seemingly suddenly disappeared. No one knows what happened to them. It's believed that at its prime 22,000 people lived here. There is speculation that drought led them to other places where they assimilated into other native cultures. To me that doesn't make sense. How could a civilization build an entire city like this and have the resolve to abandon it and move to another location? Furthermore how could there be no history of this migration and assimilation of one people group into another. Let's imagine for a moment they migrated into the Navajo or Ute society. Wouldn't their certainly be history, or at least legends, of such a large invasion of another people group. It doesn't add up to me. These people literally disappeared from Mesa Verde, leaving neither trace nor evidence, which leads me to certainly not yet believe but still entertain the thought of some sort of extraterrestrial intervention. Call me crazy, but it's also the wild imagination I have that allows to me speculate and entertain the thought. It's fun to conjure up your own theories to the matter.

Mesa Verde, unlike many National Parks, doesn't have an abundance of recreational opportunities. There are not a lot of hiking trails, and the terrain is not terribly unique in my opinion. The main attractions are these rock houses, and they justly deserve all the attention they get but, in all my experiences, this park seems more like a National Historic Site. However, curious enough, how could it be a Historic Site if we really don't know that much about the people who lived here nor a timeline of their events? It could be branded something new: a "National Mystery Park," perhaps.

Leaving Mesa Verde we headed into Durango, Colorado. A classic railroad town turned tourist hub. We walked around Main Avenue, which is lively with numerous restaurants, cafes, and shops. Most of the buildings were made of brick with arched windows, and tasteful facades that were true to the architecture of the buildings they represented. We were looking for a place to have a mid-day meal.

The downtown had a classic small town feel to it. We got distracted from seeking food to looking at t-shirts. Aunt Mary wanted a Durango t-shirt, and so we went into a few t-shirt shops. Durango had been a special place for her, because here is where they got on the historic Durango and Silverton Train to go white water rafting. Also Aunt Mary rarely gets to see her kids, as they all live so far away, so this was a special memory. I also purchased a t-shirt because although I didn't get to see much of Durango, it is where I got reunited with my aunt and cousins. That held significance.

Our mid-day meal proved to be tasty. We ate at a local brewery with very atypical and delicious burgers. I believed mine included avocado and mango. I remember my cousins had asked me how my brothers were doing. I told them about Timothy graduating from college and seeking his place in the world, and telling them about my older brother Nathan. They hadn't heard all the details of how Nathan's chocolate company, Raaka Chocolate in Brooklyn had grown into a new factory and how my brother has really become a leader in the connoisseur chocolate world.

After our meal we ran a few errands, popped into Dairy Queen for a treat, and headed back to the Airbnb where we began our package and assembly party, getting ready for the adventure the following day. We also had to clean up the place as we were checking out early the next morning and wouldn't be back. The day ended with me sitting out on the terrace with my cousins munching on the fruit and vegetable tray we had put together. The day had been full and rich, and so I relaxed in the peace of a day well spent and the anticipation of the adventure ahead.

BACKPACKING IN THE SAN JUAN MOUNTAINS

The dirt road we were traveling on was bumpy, rattling my little rental car and swinging my National Park pass hangtag side to side like a violent pendulum. It was a prime example of a washboard road, and the grooves on this road so hard they might as well have been paved. My cousin Jonathan and I were in this car trailing Paul who was in another leading the way with Mary and Ines.

We were on our way to the trailhead which would guide our adventure up into the San Juan Mountains where we would camp and visit the Ice Lakes. I had only a vague idea of what to expect because I hadn't even seen photographs of this place. I was trusting my cousin Paul with this adventure. After all, since he'd come all the way from Germany for a visit, and this hike was on his list of things to do, it must have been well researched.

We came to a small parking area nestled down in a

valley with a rushing river and a footbridge on one side and
prairie on the other. Elsewhere dark pines stood in contrast.
We were in an area managed by the National Forest Service.
There were a few other cars, but the place was by no means
busy. We quickly geared up, took a group photo, and were
on our way.

The morning was absolutely beautiful. The sky was
pure blue, the sun bright and cheerful. Vibrant colors were
painted all around– the green of the pine and prairie, the
orange and greys of the Colorado rock, the white of the left-
over snow in the high reaches, and even the bright yellow
glow of Paul's neon shirt. The sun was at such a position
and the air so clear that every wrinkle and crack of rock was
exposed, every tree top was distinguishable, and the dance
of every rustling leaf was visible. The landscape was in the

highest of definition, fully awake and alive.

The hike was about two miles. The whole thing was an incline, but it wasn't terribly steep. There were a series of switchbacks along the ascent which lessened the immediate incline. The trail by nature was not difficult but my backpack was by no means light. I was carrying a lot of water and it weighed me down, and so it made this hike pretty strenuous. I've thought back to this hike in other challenging backpacking situations. I remind myself, *If I can hike up the San Juan Mountains with that backpack, I can certainly do this.*

The hike took us on a very narrow path into a thick pine forest with lots of growth on the forest floor. At one point, near the beginning of our journey, we came to a rushing stream. We had to cross it by our own creativity. Ines took off her shoes, carefully placing her feet on stones to cross. I kept my waterproof boots on and trudged through the water. Paul leaped over. Mary and Jonathan found their own ways.

We came to a second wilder more intense crossing later on. Two logs had been placed across the rushing water, but with nothing to hold onto, it became a careful balancing act. We found two large thin pieces of tree limbs that Mary held onto on either side. She stuck them down into the rush of the water, like trekking poles, to help keep balance while crossing over.

As we ascended the mountains we came to a hybrid aspen and pine forest which opened out into a wild grass prairie on the mountain side. It reminded me of my journey up the mountain in Manti Lasal.

About halfway up our ascent we came to a waterfall just off to the side of the trail. It was loud and dropped very sharply. We were able to stand right next to it. Paul had a Go-Pro camera on a stick. We took a group photo. It was also about this time that Jonathan discovered he left a camera lens or a battery back in my car. He chose to go down to retrieve it. He ran, and it didn't take long for him to catch back up with us, but after the extra mileage he was tired.

We found a spot to take a short break. It was in an area of prairie where trees stepped aside to present a majestic view of the valley which curved around a bold mountain. The mountain in view had an exposed top of grey rock with streaks of snow painted down its side. All around and below were thick congregations of pines sharply pointing upward.

Alongside the trail, there was a rock boulder maybe fifteen feet high. Jonathan and I climbed up to the top where I was able to catch Jonathan, on camera, in a pensive pose with the mountain behind him.

After our short break we continued on our journey climbing higher and higher, the backpack straps digging deeper and deeper into our shoulders, and suddenly we reached our summit! We found ourselves in the most beautiful basin. The entire floor of this basin was covered in wildflower plants. They weren't in bloom, but they filled the air with a sweet aroma. All around were slopes of green wild grass growing up the sides of the basin. On these slopes were streams of water cascading down from ice melt. It was so fanciful, so perfect. Places like this don't seem to exist outside of fantasy. On the basin floor the streams of rushing water spread in all directions among the wild flower plants, creating a series of islands. This was all thousands of feet up

in the mountains. It was a little bowl of paradise removed from the rest of the world, elevated up here, tucked away, hidden, and we were the only ones taking it in. We had the whole basin to ourselves. And although we were clearly exposed to this realm of nature, because we were down in a basin, it felt like were sheltered in this exclusive paradise.

We chose a camping destination over by a small collection of pine trees on the far end of the basin. To get there was a bit of a trick, because the streams of water which spread out on the basin floor did so in such a wild manner. Some of these streams were wide and forceful. We had to troubleshoot numerous times, finding our way on and off numerous basin islands, backtracking when the streams were too wide for crossing.

When we made it to the pine trees there were mounds of snow protected by the shade. Among them were a few fallen trees creating places to sit down. Next to these were natural pads of pine needles and flat ground to pitch tents. Fittingly so, we set up camp. We placed our tents all relatively close to each others and next to the tall pines. Our camp was near the far end of the basin where a beautiful waterfall split as it fell, creating two side-by-side waterfalls which crashed so elegantly down against rocks and into the network of streams. At the base of the falls were a collection of shards of dark wet rocks that had crumbled down with the falling water.

Despite being out in the wild, I felt sheltered two-fold: First, we were down in a basin with the sloping walls around us placing us in our own little world. Secondly, we

were in the fold of the small patch of forest with a strong
sense of camp establishment. We had our little tent village,
or the bedrooms as I liked to call them. Next to that was a
mound of snow, were we had refrigeration– our natural
kitchen. I had taken out my water bottles and stuck them in
the snow. Next to that, was a collection of stumps, fallen
tree parts, and rock oddities creating an area to sit down and
have a fire– the natural living room, the common area.
All of this was hidden and sheltered by the cover of the
pines. Never before had nature seemed so accommodating.
It was as if it was saying, "Welcome to my finest. Make
yourself at home."

After we set up camp we went around exploring our
immediate surroundings, admiring the waterfalls, collecting

wood for a fire. During all of this exploration Jonathan was inside his tent taking a nap. He was tired from his extra hiking from having backtracked for his missing camera parts. Plus his recent sleep schedule was not his usual Air Force schedule.

I could hardly believe I was here, that this was real, that this was where we would get to spend the night, a backpacker's paradise, a deep cleansing oasis for the soul. And there was more to be seen than the wonders already set before us. Once Jonathan would awaken from his nap we would take an afternoon hike from camp up to the Ice Lakes.

When Life's Path is Frozen Over

It was the middle of the day and the moment had come. It was time to temporarily part from our camp in the San Juan Mountains and ascend to the Ice Lakes.

Jonathan had awoken from his nap. The rest of us were fully oriented to our camp surroundings and we were ready for the next leg of our adventure. The plan was to ascend, enjoy the stunning beauty, and come back down to camp later to enjoy a fire and an evening in the basin.

We knew rain was in the forecast and very likely, and beyond the basin, in the distance a dark ominous sky grew. We realized we had no time to spare. We wanted to get to the Ice Lakes before the storm knowing there is no comfort being found on top a mountain in the midst of lightning.

The trail up to the Ice Lakes was right behind our camp. It was very steep most of the time meandering up the mountainside. Much of it was covered in layers of snow and so the journey was largely a trek on top snowpack. It required us all to hunch over, balancing our weight to maintain stance on the mountain.

I had my handy trekking pole with me to dig into the snow and pull myself forward. I decided to lend it to Aunt Mary. She would have been fine without it, but I thought she could use it more than myself. She was very grateful. When I hike in a group I very much have a team mindset. We are like one unit or one creature, and so it's important to support each other to reach the goal.

At times there was question of which way to go, because we could not locate the path in the midst of all the snow. Recollecting this sparks another parallel to life. I feel that there are definite right answers to many things in life, very much so in a moral sense. In certain situations there are certain decisions which are moral and just that need to be made. These are the pathways in life which lead to certain outcomes and chains of events, but life is full of noise, of opinions, of differing views, of distractions, of complications, and sometimes these clear and definite trails become covered in our notions. We can't find them and we search and search our lives for meaning, trying to find our way. However, sometime we search life with a cold heart, and when a heart stays cold, the ice doesn't melt and there's little to no chance of finding the path. If we let our hearts break open, and allow the healing power of God to enter in and his compassion to influence our lives, it's easier for the snow or ice to melt and for us find our way.

Other times, despite our closeness to God and seeking His direction, the unwanted storms of life will not cease on our paths. It's like when a canyon forms, not by choice but by the forces around us. It's in these moments when we need to realize that we don't always need to see the path. The spirit of God leads us over the snowpack when the trail is nowhere to be seen. That spirit can move us forward when confusion is so apparent in the world around us. He guides our moral compass. But it's a matter of trust, a matter of surrendering fear, a matter of realizing you may not see where you are going, but you are not lost.

I think that is so true about my life. Some people have definite five years plans or ten year plans and they know exactly where they are going with a plan on how to get there. There's nothing wrong with that. I believe setting goals and having a vision is very important, but I've lived enough life to know that too much faith and hope in one's own plans, and especially on one's method to get there, can lead to major disappointments. Personally, I feel like much of my life is walking on top snowpack. I continue day by day seeking direction, making plans, but surrendering those plans to God. Sometimes the snow melts around me and direction becomes clear, and in those moments I savor scenery and enjoy it. Ecclesiastes 7:14 reminds us, "When times are good, enjoy them, but when times are bad, consider this: God has made one day as well as the other, and man never knows what the future may bring."

More often in life, storms leave snowpack, and I continue with trust and confidence knowing that the Spirit of God leads me. I may not always know where I am going, but I am certainly not lost.

In both a spiritual and physical sense, I find it very
rare to feel lost in life. It's an understanding that nowhere
in this world is outside the realm of God's power. He is
always with me. Even the most daunting and foreign places
are still within God's dominion. Also, spiritually and emo-
tionally, nothing escapes God's vigilance and intervention.
It reminds me of one of my favorite yet simplest bible verses, Psalm 37:4, "The angel of the Lord encamps around
those who fear him and delivers them." This especially
sticks out to me because I know what it means to
"encamp". It's traveling from one place to another, not
staying put, but finding residence in temporary places, and
so the verse doesn't say the Angel of the Lord sets up per-
manent residence at our mailing address. It says the Angel
of the Lord "encamps"– travels with us. There is nowhere
I can go in this life to fall out of the intervention of God's
protection. Even in the darkest canyons, the Angel of the
Lord will set up camp with us. On our way out of the canyon, up into our mountains, when the storm rolls in and
the snow covers the trail, the Angel of the Lord is there to
protect us and God's Spirit is there to lead. How could I
possibly ever be lost when the divine presence of God is
with me?

That is something to celebrate and put us at ease.
But it's all a choice. Some people choose to live their lives
in canyons alone. They are unwilling to acknowledge how
they've gotten there, and in their pride they attempt mountains covered in snow with no guide. As for me, I'd be
completely lost and I would not have true peace, and so

I've made another choice.

True peace also doesn't mean you never have concerns or acute worry. These things can be mechanisms to spur intelligent thinking and action, like Aunt Mary warning us "We need to turn around," as she turned to look at the deep dark ominous sky growing towards us. We were all spread out. Mary was at the end of the pack, Jonathan and I were in the middle, and Paul and Ines were somewhere up above already nearing the Ice Lakes. Mary called out numerous times with concern in her voice. Not wild and unchained fear, but intellect calling out as a mother's need to protect her family. I had paused a couple of times and wondered if we should indeed turn around, but despite her hesitation, Mary proceeded forward. We came up over a ridge and reached the Ice Lakes. It was named very appropriately, because it was all frozen over. Snow and ice was everywhere. A stream of turquoise spread across where the water was slightly warmer, and the very peak of the mountain stood up behind it covered in snow except for a few stripes of dark exposed rock. Although silly as it may sound, the best way to describe it is that it looked like were among a giant mass of cookies 'n cream ice cream.

Despite snow on the ground all around the air was not particularly cold. We were all in shorts and I was even in a tank top. In the photos it looks a little odd. It doesn't appear to make sense. In such an environment it seems like we should have been bundled up to the extreme.

We took some photos together but didn't stay long. The storm behind did look like it was approaching determinedly.

On our descent, Paul went sliding down on a portion of the snowy mountain side. It was a lot quicker and faster going down. We made it back to our camp in the basin safely.

Except for a light sprinkling, the storm never came, but the temperature changed and it became very cold. We would spend the rest of the day and evening huddled around a fire drying our wet socks and keeping warm.

A Night in the Ice Lake Basin

"Whatcha doin'?" I asked my cousin Paul, as I sat down by the fire.

"Cookin' socks," he replied.

Some people roast marshmallows, or cook hot dogs, but Paul was holding our socks over the fire, cooking socks, in attempt to dry them. The trek up to the Ice Lakes had involved lots of snow getting into our boots. Paul had found a tree branch laying around which curved in such a manner that it was perfect for laying our socks across and holding over the fire.

Everyone had volunteered their socks including myself. We also set our boots next to the fire to try and dry them. Sadly Mary's boots were a little too close and got singed.

It was early evening, but the temperature had al-

ready dropped greatly. We were all in our hoodies and jack-
ets and had our bare feet propped up against rocks next to
the fire, inviting the soothing heat to keep them warm.

Paul handed off the sock roasting responsibility to
me and went in search of more wood for the fire. It was a
very hungry fire, burning things up quickly. I found a place
to prop up the sock drying branch so I could be hands free.

We all had contributed to finding firewood and kindling but Paul won the prize for this. There was a pattern.
He'd disappear. We would carry on conversation and after a
while he would return with arms full of wood and kindling.
At one point I remember we all laughed. Paul had found an
enormous piece of tree trunk and was carrying it to camp
over his head, seemingly effortlessly, like an experienced
woodsman. He had a grin on his face seeping from his sense

of personal accomplishment, I would assume. The question on all our minds was, "where did he find that, and how did he resolve to lift it?"

"That's so Paul," Jonathan commented.

There had clearly been a place set up to have a fire prior to our arrival. Paul had taken the lead in renovating the area. He found logs and rocks and assembled them to create a bench with a backrest and armrests. We had our own living room set. Eventually everyone discovered they could put rocks close to the fire to heat them up and then remove them from the fires edge to warm their feet. I initially had the best seat. I was tucked in the corner of the makeshift bench, sitting on the log, my back resting against a broken piece of timber and my feet on a smooth rock warmed to the perfect temperature by the fire. In due time I rotated out from my comfortable corner to let someone else enjoy the

prime sitting spot.

There was still quite a bit of day left but no one had plans to leave the fire. The air around us was just too cold and wet, and some of us were sore from the hikes of carrying all our supplies for camping up the mountain and then trekking up snow to the Ice Lakes.

As we sat there poking around the fire a Marmot probably thirty feet away crawled up out of its burrow, took a few steps forward, shouted at us, and then ran back into his hole. It happened a few times. Sometimes he wouldn't make a noise but would just watch us. He was probably trying to figure out what we were and what we were doing here.

Jonathan had brought some sort of soup to cook by the fire for himself, but the rest of us just snacked on dry goods. Jonathan also heated a Clif Bar over the fire, which is a tactic I've now adopted. The bars become pleasantly soft and warm. However, they do absorb really well a smoky flavor which takes some getting used to.

After we were by the fire for many hours the conversation died down, and I decided to open a round of Would You Rather, something I learned from my younger brother, Timothy. You go around in a circle taking turns, posing ridiculous questions like "Would you rather jump out of an airplane or plummet down Yosemite Falls?"

When night had fallen and the fire turned to glowing embers, we checked into our tents for the night. I was unprepared, not knowing this would be the coldest night of my existence.

I had fallen asleep okay, but in the middle of the night I awoke freezing. I was very uncomfortable. I had only packed one sleeping bag, a small lightweight one that's packaging stated it was good for temperatures down to forty degrees. It was for sure below forty degrees. I would assume the temperature had plummeted below freezing. The sweatshirt I was wearing and my lightweight sleeping bag were not enough. I should have known better. On top of that, my head had no warmth to sink into. I had only brought my very small trunk pillow which seemed to absorb the cool air. And here I was in Kelty, my lightweight and airy tent. I should have been more prepared but, aside from the Rocky Mountains, I had spent weeks in the desert and temperatures like this were unimaginable.

There were a couple things I could do. First, I took the nylon bag which the sleeping bag is stored in and I put it over my head, trying to capture the heat of my breath. Secondly, I put my hands in my pants, for they were growing numb. There was a third option too. I could climb into another tent, but there were questions on my mind: *Would that be socially acceptable? Even if it's not, isn't it okay in dire situations like this? Is this an emergency? Will I be ok? Which tent would be the less awkward one to climb into, the tent with my Aunt Mary and Jonathan or the tent with Paul and Ines?* I unzipped my tent and looked outside contemplating going over to one of their tents. I couldn't pull myself to do it. I'll suffer, I concluded. So with my head in a bag and my hands in my pants I slept on and off, waking up cold and uncomfortable, and reminding myself that the night will end. Warmth will come in the

morning. Never before had I been happier for the morning's arrival.

That morning we didn't stay long in the basin. We
were all cold and hungry. As the others were slowly waking
up and putting themselves together I walked around camp
admiring the expanse of the basin waking up. It was beautiful. The sun was golden and caused everything that was wet
and frozen to shimmer in its light. Paul and Ines also walked
around and sat together on a fallen tree trunk, looking out
into the basin. No one said anything. I suppose we were all
taking in the awe of our surroundings and trying to thaw
out. I walked out from the shade to feel the slightest bit of
warmth falling from the sun. It wasn't much, but I'd take it.

I remember when we were packing up Jonathan was
shaking off the morning dew from his tent, neatly folding it,
making sure every corner matched. I, on the other hand, am
much more haphazard when packing my tent. I live in the
fine line between the type A and type B personalities. Tent
packing is just not on the top of my priorities. To each his
own, but I should learn to keep better care of some of my
things.

When we were all packed up we hiked back across
the basin, crossed over the streams and rivers, hiked down
the forests and prairies, and made it back to the car. I talked
with Ines a lot on the hike down. I didn't know her very
well. I had only met her briefly on a couple of family occasions. I was very pleased to get to know her. We got to talking about life in Germany and I was extended the offer to
come visit.

Back at the cars there was talk by my cousins of bathing in the river, but I knew I didn't have much time to spare and needed to get on my way. My goal was to drive seven hours to the western side of Utah, to Yuba Lake State Park. Aunt Mary and my cousins would continue their adventure on to Arches National Park. I brought out my map, spread it across the top of my car, explained some of the features worth seeing, and recommended a stop at the Moab diner.

Then it was time to part ways. It was sad to leave but I felt so thankful for the experiences shared together. From Mesa Verde to the Ice Lakes, the adventures with this bunch were truly unique and special. The memories will last with me forever.

ASSAULTED AT YUBA LAKE

"I'm going to be lost and homeless," were my thoughts. I had made the day long drive from the San Juan Mountains across Colorado to the middle of Utah to Yuba Lake State Park. On my trip I had pulled over a few times to take pictures, sat in road construction where I did some reading, and stopped to eat. Now here at Yuba Lake I knew the campground gates closed at a certain hour and I felt that I had just made it in time, but the number on my reservation didn't match any in the campground. I was running out of time. The sun was setting. The day was over. If I couldn't find my site before dark and the gates closed, what could I do?

I looped around a second and third time on the smooth black asphalt of the developed campground. A group of children, out playing with a ball, started to give me questioning looks. I had concluded there must be another campground in the park. I stopped by a bulletin board. It had a map although poorly labeled and hard to read. It looked like there was perhaps a campground on the other side of the lake and the drive did not look short. Forget my reservation, I thought. By the time I'd get there the gate would be locked. I'll just stay here, but I soon realized I couldn't. Another drive around revealed to me that the campground was full.

I felt I had only one option, to journey across to the other side of the park. I'd have to set aside my concern that the gate would be locked and work a little more diligently to find my site in the darkness of the remote Utah night, but could I do that? There was the possibility that I could end up with no place to stay, but I remembered the pictures of the campsite. It looked so beautiful. It would be a letdown if I couldn't find it.

So, my journey took me on a rough dusty unpaved road in the dark remote desert over to the other side of the lake. It took me about an hour, as I drove slowly to keep my car from falling to pieces. My cars headlights were the only light I had in the darkness of night, and I was waiting for some sort of creature to scurry in from the desert brush, into the road, in the line of visibility, but it never happened.

When I arrived there was no gate but a grouping of three or four campsites very remote and largely underdeveloped. It was evident why a gate was not needed. No one comes out this way. I was alone, an hour's drive from the next human, in the dark, somewhere in remote Utah, and next to Yuba Lake. *Okay. I dig this. This is kind of cool*, I thought. I was relieved that I found a place I could call home for the night.

I gave a sigh of relief. Then I opened my car door and was assaulted. Bugs poured in the car, flew up my nostrils, buzzed in my ear, and darted at my eyes. They were annoying little gnats and miniscule moth type creatures. I quickly closed the door and turned my air conditioning on high to blow the insects to the back of the car. These insects were fierce. I didn't notice any of them biting, so that was good, but they were overwhelmingly invasive and annoying. I guess since Yuba Lake is the only body of water for hundreds of miles out here in the desert, all the insects congregate here and have wild Vegas style parties.

I needed a clear strategy for this. I needed to minimize the number of times I'd open the car door, and I needed to set up and get in my tent the quickest way possible. I popped the trunk and swiftly went out to grab my tent and the bag with my toothbrush. I implemented my in-car toothbrushing method, which I invented in the Rocky Mountains, and then put on my head lamp. The insects immediately swarmed around the light all over my face when I opened the car door, but I figured out that they weren't drawn to the head lamp if I set it to the red light setting.

So with the red glow of my headlamp, I managed to set up my tent with such speed that you'd think my life depended on it. I threw in a pillow and a sleeping bag, and jumped in, zipping the tent closed as fast as I could. Fortunately very few insects snuck in with me, and the ones who did were quickly annihilated. I laid down and laughed. What a crazy experience. I laughed in response to the craziness of the whole situation, driving miles and miles into nowhere and getting ready for bed and setting up camp in a wild fury, but I also laughed with a giddy notion of relief. I was finally in for the night, and I was safe.

I pulled out my book on the West and red another chapter. Reading puts me at ease and keeps me company when I find myself completely alone in remote and unknown places. I discovered this when I was alone up in the remote reaches of Manti Lasal.

That night I slept very well. I made up for the lost sleep the night before in the freezing San Juan Mountains. I was able to stay asleep well into the sunrise. It's radiance warmed my whole tent, embracing me in comfort. I eventually sat up and looked out my tent window to the beautiful Yuba Lake. The sandiness of the desert hills met the pale blue of the lake, reflecting the clear sky. The insects were gone, the air was clear, and a refreshed spirit of adventure was painted in the morning sky.

I put on a pair of well-worn and ripped jeans that I rolled up to the knees and I put on my Rocky Mountain cap. I walked around the edge of the water right next to my campsite. Small waves lapped on the sandy shore while the warm sun welcomed me and introduced me to the new day.

Reflections on the Rural People of Nevada

Approaching Great Basin National Park I was driving through some serious desert in which nothing would grow. To me it appeared to be a giant salt flat. The ground was white and contrasted the blue and purple mountains in the distance. I pulled over to the side of the road to take in the scenery. I stepped out of my car and the heat was extreme.

There was no way for me to gage the distance of the expanse before me, for there were no objects to give perspective. There was nothing but a grand mirage of water. It appeared that the desert housed a great lake, but the image disappeared at certain angles and the illusion waved in the heat. I knew it was desert trickery.

I'd seen pictures of Great Basin National Park. How could its beautiful streams, glacier ponds, and pine forests appear in the midst of this? I drove further into nowhere.

No other car, business, nor home had been spotted in a long time. The desert eventually permitted low lying shrubbery, but it was still a very typical Nevada desert nonetheless. The scenery would have to make a drastic change if I was going to arrive at the park I'd seen in the pictures.

And it did. The mountains in the distance grew taller as I approached them. I knew the park had to be tucked up in the mountains. After zipping across the flat desert road, which was so inviting for high speeds, I came to a "T" in the road. An arrow pointed in both directions and a large stop sign read "WHOA!" An arrow pointed left to Baker, and another arrow also pointed left to "Great Basin National Park." There was no indication of what a right turn would yield.

I soon arrived at Baker, Nevada— gateway to the Great Basin National Park. The place consisted of people living in dilapidated trailers, an abandoned shack with a sign posted "Museum of the Future," a car which looked like it had been abandoned in the 1920s, some sort of business labeled "The Happy Outlaw," and quirky and seemingly random pieces of roadside art. There was a manikin lady's legs sticking up from the ground, as if she had plummeted or was pulled into the Nevada desert. Another piece featured an alien in a wheelchair adorned with old electronics and parts of appliances. This is so weird, I thought. I like this. This is so Nevada.

I am an outsider to Nevada, and from my outsider perspective here is how I see it: Rural Nevada residents embrace their weirdness. They even showcase it, and irony is their forte. Things don't always have to make sense for them. They don't have to have a theme or message. You just shoot for random and strange, but throw in some irony

Museum of the Future

when possible, and that is pleasing, such as the abandoned shack labeled "Museum of the Future."

This is not just an observation based on Baker. Elsewhere in Nevada I've seen some interesting sites. Once I stopped at a gas station, and in the men's room, I relieved myself into a cascading urinal fountain adored with rocks and greenery, where people had thrown pennies in, as if making a wish. Also outside of Death Valley, on the Nevada side, in the abandoned city of Rhyolite I'd seen the figures of the last supper recreated as life-size ghost statues. Nevada is just full of surprises. I mean, in Baker you don't get a stop sign, you get a "WHOA!" sign. They just have to be different.

When I come across these rough looking trailers isolated in the desert, it's not something I look down on or fear. I don't think these people are hostile, nor unrelatable by any means. Some may be living in poverty, and life may not be ideal, but for many, this is just how they live in Nevada. Many people have moved to Nevada and have chosen to live here in this way. It's so far isolated from the rest of the country that sometimes these lots of land don't have access to the full array of utilities, and there's no one around to build a house hundreds of miles out in the desert. So, the only option is to resort to a trailer.

Another thing worth mentioning in my observations about rural Nevada is the fascination with the supernatural and extraterrestrial. The supernatural fascination, I think, is tied back to all the ghost towns they have. These ghost towns have held so much life and so many stories, and then they were suddenly abandoned after the silver rush, but the stories live on or are speculated. And so in these places that have been abandoned there are allusions of the past that are almost seeable and believable, just like the mirage of water in the desert. It's as if the beating heart of Nevada is a ghost itself, but a ghost really wouldn't have a beating heart, would it? That's just a piece of Nevada irony for you.

The extraterrestrial fascination may have in part to do with the mysterious Area 51 housed in the state and the vast claims of UFO sightings in the area. But also, when you are isolated hundreds of miles out in the desert with not a soul to talk to and the heat is really getting to you, I could imagine your mind might convince you of, or conjure up stories of alien encounters.

However, when it comes to Nevada, I love it! There's

nothing like it.

When I arrived at the park boundary, I didn't stop at the park visitor center. My priority was to secure a campsite in the Wheeler Peak Campground. I proceeded straight up the mountain, where the landscape changed into a dry pine forest. I was able to secure a great campsite within a small patch of trees. Like Nevada itself Great Basin National Park is full of surprises and is an underrated gem. It would become one of my new favorite National Parks! I wouldn't say stop here and check it out, I'd say, "Whoa!, have. a. look!"

The Greatness of Great Basin

I rested in my tent, and I mean truly rested. There had not been any other moment in my life in which I felt as calm as I did that evening in my tent in Great Basin National Park.

When I arrived earlier in the day I looped around Wheeler Peak Campground twice, looking for a vacant site. The campground seemed to be full, but eventually I struck success and found a perfect site.

This was a developed campground and so the road was paved. There was a place to park my car, and my campsite had a picnic table and a fire ring. As an added bonus, this particular site had a patch of pine trees, and within the patch of trees was a flat barren area to pitch my tent. I could camp in my own miniature forest in the welcoming shade. This would be greatly appreciated after having spent most of the day in the hot desert sun.

This little forest gave me a feeling of privacy and security, despite the dead squirrel in there, just a few feet from
where I pitched my tent. Flies buzzed around it. I made a
mental note to make sure to avoid it. The last thing I wanted to do was to clean fresh juicy squirrel guts from my hiking boots or feel them ooze onto the sides of my flip
flops. It hadn't crossed my mind that the real concern
should be the carcass attracting other animals.

After I set up camp I went for a hike taking the trail
which began in the campground. The campground was
named after Wheeler Peak because the mountain peak towered over it. The trailhead led to the peak, but the trailhead
also veered to Stella Lake and Teresa Lake, both small lakes
at the bottom of the rock glacier. I took in these two lakes

and saved the hike to Wheeler Peak for the following day.

Up here above the Great Basin Desert the forest was warm and spacious. Pine needles, fallen tree limbs, and streams covered the forest floor so beautifully. I made my way through the forest, observantly, with a full sense of wonder. This type of open forest was new to me. *What sort of animals live here? What sort of plants and features might I expect to see?* The trail eventually led to Stella Lake. I stood there alone. The bright sun shone down, and the landscape opened up to a pristine view.

Except for a few patches of snow, I saw crumbled rock spread all over the landscape amidst clusters of pines. It was evident that all the rocks had fallen over time from the focal point. Just beyond the pines in the far reaches it towered: Wheeler Peak, in all its majesty with a prominent rock glacier cascading from its height. This was the Great Basin National Park I had seen in pictures. Looking down, the water was turquoise, stealing blue from the clear sky and reflecting green from the pines surrounding it. Up close the water was very clear. I could see jumbled rocks just on the other side of the gentle water. Who would have ever guessed that up here hidden in the heights beyond the heat of the desert was such a place. What else is Nevada hiding up in its mountains?

This lake before me was not very big. It was small. I could easily swim from one side to the other. It seemed more like a pool. That combined with the fact that the pine trees weren't terribly tall, the rocks around had fallen in relatively small fragments, and the only wildlife I had observed were chipmunks playfully running around, gave this place a sort of miniature feel. This sensation was appealing. It made the place welcoming, homey, and manageable. It was like I had come upon a secret, exclusive, pocket-sized Montana.

It seemed as if the forest of the park was only possible because of Wheeler Peak. Here at the base of this giant rock feature was the collection of its ice melt, the fruit of its shade. It created the conditions for this pristine forest, another paradise hidden in the high reaches of a mountain.

Sometimes in our spiritual lives the greatest places of pristine serenity are up in high reaches, well beyond the canyons in which so many people dwell. It takes initiative and determination to get to these places. Sometimes it involves making it past the desert of life in which everything seems so fruitless and barren. In other instances it might mean walking over the snowpack, with not a trail in site, but relying on the guidance of God's spirit. When you're traversing your mountain you may not see these secret places hidden up in the high reaches, but they will surprise you if you endure.

It's important to say that arriving at these places of peace in life requires you to be well elevated from your canyons. It may be that you are stuck in a canyon of addiction, of insecurity, of selfishness, of anger, or of any ailment. Places of peace may not be found until you make your way up into the mountains. If you are stuck below in the canyon, you've got to ask yourself what is it going to take for you to get to your place of peace? Forgiveness? Admittance? Reliance? What about all of these?

Life is not easy, but we all long for places of peace. I also want to be free flowing and pure like the little streams of water that flowed from the mountain lakes into Lehman Creek. They flowed smoothly and quickly, just with a subtle trickling sound, and they meandered and swerved through the forest clear and cool– not a care. Their flow was level to the ground around it. They weren't carving out canyons, stirring up trouble, but flowed right along with the landscape of life. I remember holding my camera to take some pictures and thinking, *I've never seen water flow more beautifully in my life.*

My hike had been extremely pleasant, with the company of the sweet pines, the warm and gentle dry air around me, the vibrant blue and green colors of the ice melt water, the captivating vista of Wheeler Peak, the pine cones and pine needles spread all across the forest floor, chipmunks scurrying about, birds singing in the trees, and the subtle trickle of water meandering through the forest.

When I got back to camp I felt, in a sense, high. It felt like nature had just shot something sedating through my veins. Maybe it was the altitude, or perhaps I was just tired and relieved from the desert. Or maybe it was the gift of a beautiful landscape and the exercise in the forest that released endorphins.

I sat down on my sleeping bag in my tent, tucked in between the pines, and I was at perfect blissful ease. I brought my water bottle and my book on the West in with me. I took a sip of my water and laid down. The sleeping bag felt soft, silky, and warm, as it slid under my skin of my

arms and brushed against my heels. Beneath it was the comfort of my air mattress filled full. I stretched my legs out and
I could almost hear them giving off a sigh of relief. My head
sunk heavily into my pillow. I looked up through the top of
my tent into the limbs of the pine trees. Just beyond them
were the rich blue sky and a few clouds lingering. *I could gaze
at this view for hours,* I thought.

The lighting was perfect in my tent, coming in pro-
portionally on all sides of the white tent, making my skin

almost appear as if it was glowing that dusty red of southern Utah. The greenness of my sleeping bag was illuminated by the light, complementing the color of the pines overhead. I was relaxed, but my senses were keen and aware.

The temperature here was perfect. The air was deeply breathable and the sides of my tent subtly radiated heat. I felt perfect, wrapped up in the womb of nature which was going to birth my rejuvenation. I broke open my book and started to read. Then I fell deep asleep.

I woke up in the early night. I hadn't expected to fall asleep and sleep so long and so deeply. I thought about just staying put in the tent, but concluded I really needed to eat. So I lifted myself up, stepped out of my tent, walked through my little forest and over to the other end where I built a fire in the ring. I gathered up as much warmth from it as I could, because the air had grown cool. I cooked some oatmeal and ate whatever other snacks I had. I wrote a few postcards and then called it a night. I walked back into my mini-forest and zipped myself into my tent for a night of deep rejuvenating sleep.

SUMMITING WHEELER PEAK

I looked up at the mountain. *I don't know about this,* I thought. I had never summited something quite like this before. This was Wheeler Peak in Great Basin National Park, at 13,065 feet. It was bold and bald. Nothing grew on its mountain top.

The guys in the Rock the Park show, which I had become so accustomed to watching, didn't make it to the top. They turned around in their Great Basin episode, but they had tried it in the winter, in the snow. I had the summer advantage.

I stood there in a prairie along the mountain side among bunchgrass and black sage looking up at the mountain peak. The view looked like Wheeler Peak and the adjoining peaks used to all be connected at a higher point, all composing one grand mountain, but over time that higher summit crumbled to pieces and formed the rock glacier. Nevertheless Wheeler Peak stands very tall. It's Nevada's highest peak. Although just summiting the beast alone seemed impossible, one of my questions was, do I have time? I was not getting an early start. It was well into the afternoon.

I had started the day sitting at the Mather Overlook which is just a pullout from the main park road. I drove down there early and had a peaceful morning reading some of my book about the history of the National Park Service while fittingly sitting there next to a plaque in honor of Stephen Mather, the first director of the National Park Service. I then proceeded back down to the lower lands of the park where I cleaned out my car at a dump station. I was waiting for my scheduled tour of Lehman Caves.

"What's your favorite National Park," the park ranger asked each member of the group before our tour.

"Death Valley," I shared without hesitation.

"Alrighty," she said, as she would say after completing or beginning every sentence. She also had an accent that was very indistinguishable. It's a shame I remember more about the rangers speech patterns than the actual Lehman Caves. But the tour was very pleasant. I enjoyed it.

After the tour I ate a sandwich in the cafe right next to the Lehman Caves Visitor Center. A little standalone placard in the middle of my table read, "Ask a park ranger about ghost towns of Nevada." *I most certainly will,* I thought, considering I would be traveling all across the state on Highway 50, and ghost towns fascinate me.

After lunch I drove back up to the higher reaches of the park and eventually found myself geared up, looking at the towering Wheeler Peak and trying to decide if I should hike it. I tried to imagine where the trail might lead and tried to visualize it before me on the landscape. It looked like it made its way through the sparse forest of pinyon and juniper with granite out crops and prairie until it reached the spine of an exposed ridge, which gradually climbed until it hit a secondary base of the mountain, where a steep incline would begin around the back of the mountain. The total elevation gain would be 3,000 feet, not terrible yet significant, especially since nearly all of it was completely exposed.

Wheeler Peak

Welp, I'm here. I concluded it was time to give it a try. I figured the worst thing that could happen is that I'd have to turn around and come back or be blown off the mountain by extreme winds. Actually the latter I could have never imagined!

On my way through the prairie I spotted a group of wild turkey and some deer. On the other side of the prairie growth became sparse except for a tree every once in a while jutting up from shambles of granite.

Eventually there was nothing left except me on the

slanted fields of rock crumble. The trail evolved into switchbacks, and since the landscape was so uniform, it was difficult at times to know exactly where the trail was supposed
to be.

I reached a point where I could look down to my left
and see Teresa and Stella Lakes as miniature little puddles
below. To my right I looked out on the desert expanse of
Nevada. Directly behind me I saw the spine ridge and the
forest I had traversed, and in front of me there was just
more rock leading up to the peak

Then it hit me, the realization of just how high up I
was. It was disorienting. I'd never had such a clear 360 de-
gree view at such an elevation. Also the way the landscape
was not strictly in terms of vertical or horizontal orienta-

tion, but mountain ridges and landscapes were at odd diagonals, crooked yet beautiful, made me feel uneasy. I began to feel a bit dizzy and my heart began to beat a little extra fast on top of what was already needed for this strenuous hike.

Just a little further up the mountain the wind was gusting. It made the loose fitting parts of my hoodie flap against me violently. It blew into my ears so forcefully that it hurt. I pulled my hood over my head and held it tight, pinching it at the bottom so it wouldn't blow off. It wasn't enough to protect my ears. I had to turn my head sideways to evade the harsh gusts, and then I had to get low. When I stood tall I felt my knees switching between wobbling and clenching, trying to maintain stance.

There was sincere concern that the wind would blow me off the mountain, that I could go flapping in the wind, tossed around and dropped somewhere out in the desert below. It didn't help that throughout the course of the year I had been having repeated nightmares involving the wind. In each one I'd be walking across the Brooklyn Bridge in New York and the wind would be so powerful it would always blow something valuable out of my hands, and then the wind would wisp me off the bridge and I'd fall down into the cold water of the Hudson. No fun. It all stems back to one December on the Brooklyn Bridge when the wind did try to steal a backpack right off my back. As it had been ripped off me into the air I held on by one strap and was able to pull it back down. That event left a scarring impression on me.

But here on Wheeler Peak this wasn't just imagined.

The wind was extreme and I could feel it trying to move my body. So I proceeded up the mountain in a somewhat pitiful manner, reminding myself of Gollum from Lord of the Rings crawling over rocks, never quite standing up fully.

When I reached the top the wind had dissipated greatly. I was stunned by the view. Hundreds of miles of Nevada was visible in all directions. Here I could truly see just how mountainous Nevada was with mountains all over in the near and far reaches, with sharp points and slanted slopes, snow caps and hidden forests, and valleys of desert between them all covering great expanses. Just across from Wheeler peak was another peak that rose on a mountain which looked like it had been sliced by a knife with such a shark direct cut down to its base.

The sky up here was a very profound blue. It seemed as if I was elevated into a different atmosphere. When I looked out in the distance I could see a layer of lighter slightly murkier sky below, and I could see clouds in some far reaches that were well below where I was standing. As silly as it may sound it felt like space was just a stone's throw away.

Up here there were two little topless shelters made from rocks stacked on top of each other. I imagined they were for people to camp in. I went inside and wanted to rest for a minute and look out the structure door into the world below, but I didn't trust these structures to hold up, especially if more wind was to come. I didn't want rock collapsing on me. In one of these structures there was a mailbox stuck in the rocks. In it was a notebook— a log for people to record their accomplishment of summiting the peak. Many people had filled it with Bible verses. I supposed they were inspired spiritually by such a view and height as this.

It's spiritually affirming to reach a mountain top. It puts all of existence into focus. When you look down and ahead on the far reaches you realize just how small your problems really are. And when you accomplish the task of reaching a mountain top it reveals to you in a spiritual sense that you can get out of your canyons, traverse the desert, and reach the mountain top.

I also think mountain tops are places of hope and a taste of eternity— a place of beauty where we can look back on our lives, complete, and see what we have endured and how we fit into a bigger picture. You see many of us, on our journey's from the canyons and deserts of life into the mountains, find places of peace that God has hidden and given to us on the journey, like the little pristine forest hidden in the Great Basin National Park. But the mountaintop itself, the very peek, is something that I believe can't be reached in this life. The mountaintop is the pinnacle and completion of existence, a place of utter fulfillment, which we reach only when our time in this world is up and our souls have been accounted for. It's the completion. It is the destination. And life's entire journey in this world is preparing and leading us to it.

So in this life when we physically reach these mountaintops they are appealing and satisfying to the soul. They inspire us because they are a taste of an eternity and completion that we all naturally long for.

They also reflect the beauty of God and remind us that there is far more to existence than what we cling so tightly to in the world below

BECOMING UNWAVERING

After summiting Wheeler Peak, on the trail back to the campground, the sun was winding down to a relaxing golden glow and deer stood gracefully along the prairies edge. I stopped in the open prairie and just observed the mountain. I listened. I thought maybe it had something to say.

I observed how, despite there being a rock glacier crumbling down from its center, the sides of the mountain were firm and defined. They weren't going anywhere and they appeared to me almost as pillars.

Although it is a stretch of association, the mountain spurred me to start considering pillars and their purpose. Pillars are designed to hold things up. They support. They are dependable and unwavering. I thought about how I wanted to be like a pillar, how I desired to be a person that is supportive of others, who holds them up and is dependable.

Returning from my thoughts to capturing more of the scenery around me, I observed how the mountain is very bold despite erosion and the rock glacier. It's still not going anywhere. This mountain is firm, steady, resolute, and then I began unpacking the word that would last and linger with me— unwavering.

It's been my observation in life that consistency in a person is rare to find. People come and go. They change, they disappoint, and the slightest variation in weather can even disrupt a person. I do not want to be this type of person. I want to stand strong. I want to be a person others can rely on– a constant, a non-variable, dependable, and above all unwavering.

I want to be defined by a moral character that is unwavering, a reliability that goes without question, and I want to possess a hope that can withstand any storm.

My mind naturally began to consider my relations. Who would benefit from my unwavering stance? There weren't many people in my life I thought, but then I considered the six hundred little eyes and ears that see and hear me throughout the week. I felt the heaviness of many of their situations— fatherless homes, drugs in the house, abusive parents, inconsistencies strewn all over. Certainly not all, but a considerable number of my students are exposed to such things. It breaks my heart, but it also helps me realize my importance and potential for influence.

I recalled a dream I had on the last day of school: I dreamt that I was teaching a class. I was writing something on the whiteboard and when I turned around to address the class all the students were gone, and all the colorful decorations of my classroom were missing. The classroom was empty. I felt a terrific horror as I ran to the front office, stumbling on my way.

"They're gone! All the students disappeared!" I said. Office staff came down to my classroom.

"They are still there," one confirmed with sincere concern.

Everyone returned to a normal day's work but for me, I couldn't. My students were gone and I felt a grave sense of emptiness.

I thought long and hard about this dream. I realized that one day I will look out into an empty classroom and my career will be over and complete. What will it mean? How will the time have been spent? What is each year marked by?

Sometimes I get caught up in the mundane tasks of teaching: reaching evaluators deadlines, completing grad school busy work, entering grades into frustrating computer programs, dotting all my "i"s and crossing all my "t"s. At a mark of completion we can talk about the grades achieved and the number of students reaching the desired growth. goal. That is all good, but I think there is an opportunity for greater meaning here.

Beyond the academics, when the classroom is empty and lives have moved on, I want to know that despite the storms of life I have been an unwavering example for my students of a steady presence, dedication, moral character, and hope.

This moment in Great Basin National Park would change my career. Just months prior I spent a lot of time considering whether I was happy or not at work and if I should seek moving on to a position elsewhere, but this made me realize that my influence and potential in my current position was far greater than what I had considered and that it was much greater than my present feelings. I realized, in my new perspective, I would find greater purpose and joy in my work.

Returning to normal life I would fully adopt this word *unwavering,* let it define me, and consider it in all aspects of my life. Beyond the classroom this word led me to become better at keeping my word to friends and acquaintances. It would also motivate me to seek deeper understanding of God's promises and truly take their meanings to heart, which would keep me unwavering in hope and persistent in the midst of storms.

I am glad that evening in Great Basin I stopped to listen to the mountain, for that mountain changed me.

WELCOME TO AMERICA'S LONELIEST HIGHWAY

"You can just pull over to the side of the road and camp anywhere…" explained the park ranger as I told him about my plans to cross Highway 50, the loneliest highway in America. "…It's generally accepted," he continued.

He pulled a map out from under his desk. It was folded like a standard brochure, but he unfolded it again and again until the whole state of Nevada covered his desk. I had taken the advice from the little placard on the table in the cafe the day before which read, "Ask a park ranger about Nevada ghost towns." The ranger had explained how to get to the abandoned town of Hamilton, and he pointed out another place on the map. "That one is on private land now. There's a mining company that owns it, but you still might be able to see some of the buildings."

My plan was to cross Highway 50 to Lake Tahoe on the far west side of the state. I wanted to camp at Berlin-Ichthyosaur State Park to break up the journey and see the

ghost town that park preserved. I was asking the ranger if
there were any other ghost towns worth a stop along the
way, and if he thought I'd be able to find a vacant campsite
at Berlin-Ichthyosaur. He was an older, friendly man, who
equipped me with the you-can-do-this—it'll-be-an-
adventure kind of spirit. So, out of the Great Basin National
Park visitor center I left with my map of Nevada in hand
along with some exclusive knowledge on ghost towns. I was
excited to have them both.

Bristlecone Pine

This morning I awoke early and took a stroll through the Bristlecone Pine forest in Great Basin National Park. The park is home to the oldest trees in the world, Pinus Longaeva, the Bristlecone Pine. The oldest one was removed from the park in 1964 at 4,900 years old. Today still many ancients stand in the grove next to Wheeler Peak. They only grow at an altitude between 9,000 to 11,500 feet. Here they have found their niche, where they aren't disrupted. They are slow growing, and often as the National Park Service puts it "out-competed." So they have, in a sense, retreated to conditions in which other trees can't survive.

A short interpretive hike tells you the names and ages of the trees. What fascinates me about such old trees is putting them in context of history and considering all of the things they out date, such as all modern wars and the birth of Jesus. They precede the rise of the Roman empire. They might have been standing back during the rule of King Tut. These trees have stood through much of the milestones and tumult of the world.

Looking at them you wouldn't guess their age. They are rather girthy but not that tall in comparison to something like the Sequoia or Redwood, which we often equate with age. Their branches are unique as they twist and curve like strings of warm taffy. Once you fully consider how old they are, they start to look elderly. Their exterior is painted many different shades of brown and the trunks and limbs are brushed with indentations and grooves, like a wrinkly old man who's spent too many days out in the sun. At the same time the way they look is almost fanciful. Although extremely still and sturdy, the dramatic twisted growth and exotic posture make these trees appear frozen in mid-dance, manipulated by some strange sorcery.

Nevada never ceases to amaze me. I wouldn't have thought the world's oldest trees resided in such a place. As I closed my car door and spread out my new map on my driver's seat I was gearing up to see what other surprises this state held in the middle of its expanse. I buckled up, programed my GPS, plugged in my camera to charge, and… realized I needed gas.

As a courtesy of the National Park Service the park map labeled the location of the nearest gas station— or might I say the only gas station around. It was in Baker, Nevada, the town in the desert at the foot of the park. When I arrived I was very skeptical. There was neither a building nor a sign. There was just a single pump next to an old lamp post and a garbage can in the middle of a gravel lot. It looked to me like the remnants of an old gas station that used to stand here. Maybe I could mark this off as my first ghost town experience of the trip. Maybe this gas station predated the Bristlecone Pines.

I double checked my map. This was it. I pulled up to the pump and got out of my car into the oppressive heat and dead silence. Sure enough there was a credit card reader. The pump was functional. I was sincerely surprised and found the whole situation comical. This part of Nevada was truly a foreign place to me. I filled up, knowing that while traveling across what's called "America's loneliest highway," gas would be sparse.

A Raven's Warning:
Exploring The Ghost Town of Hamilton

A band of wild horses galloped through the sagebrush to my left. To my right the dirt road crumbled off into a ravine. The sun was bright and hot and I was out here by myself. *If something happens to my car I'm done for. Stranded in the scorching desert miles from anybody, this would be it.* I had taken the unnamed and barely marked road from America's Loneliest Highway, Highway 50, further into the remoteness of Nevada, seeking the ghost town of Hamilton.

If the park ranger at Great Basin National Park hadn't told me about this ghost town there would be no chance I would have found it, and I would have never attempted route on this wild terrain road. It was barely a road. It was more like a path just worn over in the resemblance of a road with ruts and holes, and parts of the path crumbling off and falling to the wayside. It meandered through the foothills of Mount Hamilton ever so roughly. Though I explained to the ranger that I was driving just a compact car he told me I should be fine, and he said it with such dismissing confidence that I trusted him.

A few times I considered turning around back to Highway 50 but eventually I realized I couldn't. There wasn't enough space anywhere to turn around, with the hill on one side and a ravine on the other. I was in this until the end.

Eventually the hills gave way to a wide valley and I came upon the ruins of Hamilton. The ruins were largely spread out and very diverse. I parked my car over to the side of the dirt road and first came upon the remnants of a stone house. Flat smooth stone had been stacked on top of each other to create a building but now only two adjacent walls remained. One had an arched doorway still intact that was held in place by bricks seeming to defy the laws of gravity.

In the near vicinity were other ruins of stone houses left barely recognizable in piles of rock. Further in I came upon some wooden structures. There were two buildings completely dilapidated except for their roofs just lying on the ground pointing upward.

In a field large rested a collection of enormous iron

gears with the insignia of Denver, Colorado, U.S.A. on them. My guess was that they were a part of mining equipment. In my later investigation I learned Hamilton used to be a booming silver town with a population of 12,000 at its peak in 1869. Two hundred mining companies were set up in the area. Hamilton boasted close to one hundred saloons and sixty general stores, along with dance halls and skating rinks. However, the silver deposits were found to be very

shallow, and that along with a destructive fire in 1873 led to
eventual abandonment.

As I walked around I observed large mining cars
twice as big as anything I had seen by abandoned mines in
Death Valley. From the size of the equipment I knew that at
least one of the mining operations here must have been very
large scale.

Continuing to wander around I came upon abandoned pickup trucks and a steel-frame warehouse structure
that didn't look terribly old at all. It was in definite rough
shape but it still had a large garage door intact and all exteri-
or walls standing complete. I walked through a door frame.
Inside I could see bullet holes all over the walls of the interi-
or where insulation was peeling and falling. A two story
building within the building had ominously broken glass
windows. I looked up and the roof of the warehouse had
holes every so often, evenly distributing light throughout
the building. To me the place seemed to be an abandoned
repair garage. The concrete floor was dusty and dirty and
large empty tanks, tin barrels, and appliances littered the
floor. I took a few steps in slowly.

This building, although filthy, would not be a bad
place to squat, I thought. The last thing I wanted was to encounter some insane squatter or modern day criminal hiding
out here. I stood still and quiet and just moved my head
around to observe. Then suddenly I jumped as a raven hiding up in the rafters let out a loud cry. That was enough of a
bad omen for me. Something about the place did not sit
well with me.

To add to the creepiness of the place, leaving the warehouse I walked over to a small one room wooden shack where in the doorframe hung a noose. *What is going on?* First an ominous warehouse, then a raven giving warning, and now a noose hung from a door frame.

I looked down and something small was shining bright gold in the sunlight. I brushed some dust and dirt away to reveal a small bullet shell. On the end two initials were carved. I had all intention to investigate what the initials might mean, but the golden bullet shell was lost and the initials forgotten. What came to mind at first was Kissin' Kate Barlow from Louis Sachar's book, *Holes*. She was an infamous outlaw of the Wild West and in the movie she carved her name on the canister of her bullets.

Despite the Ravens startling cry, I was not too afraid

to be here. Instead I was captivated by the mystery of it. All the ruins told a story and I was trying to figure it out. I knew nothing about Hamilton, so here I was trying to put the pieces together. *What were all these buildings? Why are some seemingly so much newer than others? Why was this place abandoned? What are all these pieces of equipment lying around?* When I observed these large gears and other equipment oddities I imagined for a second they were the ruins of an alien spaceship crash, those same aliens depicted in the petroglyphs all through Utah and Colorado and the ones rumored to be in the sky above Nevada.

My last stop in Hamilton was at the Hamilton Cemetery. Tombstones were dated from the 1870s to 1890s. One portion of the cemetery was enclosed in a gothic style short steel fence, something that looked like it had come right out of the backyard of Disney's Haunted Mansion.

Another portion of the cemetery had uniform white headstones. I noted two bared the last name of Paul, both were children who died in infancy in the 1890s. One really stuck out as it looked like nobody bothered digging a grave but rather buried the corpse in a pile of bricks and then propped the headstone up by shoving it down in the pile. It looked like at any moment a skeleton's arm would reach up in desperation from the piles of bricks.

The road I traveled on to arrive here kept going further and I wanted to see where it led, but as I drove, maybe an eighth of a mile further, my car almost got stuck in a rut. I decided I needed to turn around. My visit to Hamilton was very satisfying. It filled me with good wonder and mystery, and I took back a collection of great photos as a perfect souvenir.

How I Relate to Ghost Towns

There's something about ghost towns that's very appealing to me. It has a lot to do with the hidden stories they possess. It fascinates me to think about what life was like in these places– to realize children were born here, people were married, men toiled in the mines, and drama erupted in the saloons. People were carefully investing, gaining fortune and losing it, and some looked out their windows and pondered their existence and direction in life. And now it's all forgotten, abandoned, nothing.

It's a very humbling experience to walk around a ghost town. It reminds me of the fleeting nature of life and this world. As I was wandering around the ghost town of Hamilton in rural Nevada I was thinking of how this was the focal point of so many people's lives. They stepped out their doors and this was their world. People competed here for power and status and were so concerned with the local dealings of the mine and town, yet now it's nothing. This all helps me refocus and consider what is most important in life. At then end of the day my physical world, the buildings, the belongings, even the problems I get wrapped up in may be gone and forgotten. Even my name in this world may be lost. But the one thing that stays true and eternal is the soul. If there's anything worth investing in, it is that.

Along with this reminder of where to place life's greatest concerns, I also relate to ghost towns on a whole different level. Imagine for a moment my mind is a giant map, and in that map there are booming cities of success and progress. These are my most recent creative ideas, endeavors, and projects in completion. But also among those cities are ghost towns, vestiges of my past. These are the locations of dreams left abandoned and stories I never finished. As a writer there have been many writing projects I spent much time with. I built places and characters in my mind only to move onto better ideas, leaving those places frozen in imagination, never complete, not developed any further. Bits and pieces of them melt and wear away from memory with time. And apart from writing, there are dreams for my life in which I spent so much time putting in place the framework and foundations to make them happen, but eventually leaving them abandoned in time, and moving on with life.

In a similar way ghost towns remind me of lost friendships. Forming friendships is a lot like building houses. You create a foundation in which you form trust. From there you build walls in which to house shared memories and experiences, but as friendships fail or people leave those buildings are left unmaintained, and memories are found littered around as rare relics, or gone altogether. I suspect that for many people there are even those special people whom you loved deeper than others, whom you shared elaborate dreams with. You didn't just build houses, you built cities with them. Your dreams were expansive and seemingly so reachable, and then one day the person who was held so dear was gone, abandoning a whole network of buildings and pathways, stories, and dreams.

Such failed relationships and abandoned dreams in life have left the map of my soul with a series of ghost towns. Revisiting them can bring back a bit of bitter sweet nostalgia, but sometimes I suppose there is a raven up in the rafters warning not to enter, because some places in life are just not meant to be revisited. These ghost towns, although sometimes not wise to revisit and dwell in, in the end and in the grand scope of things are not bad. They aren't always a part of the canyonlands, rather they are spread from the deserts up into the mountainsides as a part of life's upward journey to the mountain top. You have learned from them to build better, wiser, and stronger.

When I pull open my map and see the ghost towns of life's journey they are reminders of progress. And despite moments of tragedy and heartache, when the thought of dreaming again seems impossible, dreams somehow always find a way back into life.

My journey along Highway 50 in Nevada was one of visiting ghost towns. As I left Hamilton I drove the twelve

rough miles back to Highway 50 and was relieved to get
back to a paved road. Forty five miles later I rolled into the
grand metropolis of Eureka, population 610. In Eureka,
Highway 50 turns into Main Street where one finds a hybrid
ghost town and functioning county seat. I parked on Main
Street and went for a walk. I found a brochure that led me
on a self-guided tour of the downtown, taking me past the
elegant Eureka Opera House, abandoned saloons, the hollow yet historic Colonnade Hotel, and other gems of the
Wild West.

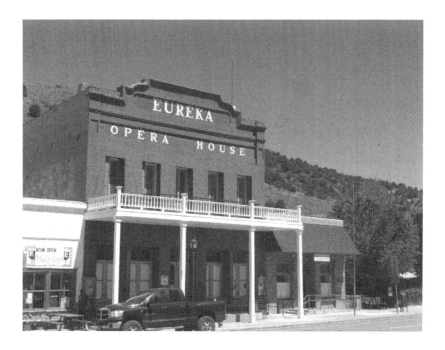

I finished my stroll with a visit to a Rains Market, a
small grocery store on Main Street. I stepped inside and was
greeted with classic Nevada. Of course it wasn't enough for
Rain's to just be a grocery store. It had to be a little above

and beyond in a Nevada sort of way. It had taxidermied animals all along the walls above the shelves. There were deer, mountain goats and lions, and fish. Later, when I was looking at Google Maps I noticed the place is labeled Rains Market and Wildlife Museum. How fitting.

The end of my first full day of Highway 50 explorations ended fifty miles south of the highway, beyond a dirt road, in Berlin-Ichthyosaur State Park. The park preserves the ghost town of Berlin which was built around a gold and silver mine, as well as undisturbed fossil remains of an Ichthyosaur, a giant marine reptile.

Before leaving Great Basin National Park in the morning I was concerned I might not find a vacant campsite, but I was the only one here. I set up my tent and

Berlin, Nevada

then went for a walk around the ghost town.

Just like in Eureka there was a pamphlet that led me on a self-guided tour but this one was hand written and copied. It told the history and significance of each building, explained how the mining system worked, told of how many young men who came to work the mines lived in a bunk house, how at its boom it had a population of just 250, yet they still had a town prostitute. It guided me to the mine supervisor's house, the machine shop, and a big old mill. Each building was furnished but in a haphazard un-kempt way, as if one day people got up and left and every-thing was abandoned as is and became worn with time. Alt-hough the buildings were blocked off from entry I could look inside and see the titles of books left on the shelves and read the containers of products left around. It was fasci-nating.

When I was on the small hill next to the machine shop I looked behind me at the desert expanse and the tall nameless Nevada mountains in the distance, warmly glowing in the evening sun. I imagined the young men who left everything, or had nothing, and came here to toil in the mines. I found the view before me beautiful, but they would have looked at it through different lenses. They probably had resentment for this landscape of inescapable deathly heat and lonely remoteness.

There was a little pathway next to the shop leading further up the hill. I wanted to see what I could find further up but as I walked, a snake slithered on the path before me. I was done. I drove back to my campsite which was beautifully located at a plateau's edge, overlooking the desert valley and out to the mountains in the distance. I took a short walk from my campsite to the building housing the grand Ichthyosaur. The building was locked but I could look inside and see the fossils. On the outside of the building on the wall was a large mural of an Ichthyosaur which I took my picture with, realizing this a once in a lifetime opportunity. Where else could I get my picture with an Ichthyosaur except in the middle of Nevada? And when would I be back?

When I walked back to my campsite the sun was setting. I listened to the utter silence of the land. I got ready for bed and looked up at the sky. If aliens were going to abduct me, this would be an ideal time and location. There would be no witnesses near nor far. I climbed into my tent with my atlas, studying routes and trying to figure out exactly how my summer adventure was going to end in the short days ahead. I had plans to go to San Francisco, but for the past few days that plan didn't sit well with me. I couldn't say why exactly, but I considered other routes and places to go. As I looked over my atlas it wasn't long before I was sound asleep in the peace of remote Nevada.

THE PLAGUE AT LAKE TAHOE

"We just need to let you know that this is the last night the campground will be open for the season, due to the plague," the host advised from her drive thru check in booth. She reached out her window, handing me a packet of papers. "We are required to give you this information about the plague."

I'll admit, I didn't know what exactly the plague was. I thought it was just a very generic term used to describe a sickness that spread quickly, or that it was some sort of medieval illness. What was she doing talking about the plague here at Lake Tahoe?

"Just make sure you stay away from rodents, especially any dead ones." My mind flashed back to the dead squirrel lying beside my tent in Great Basin National Park.

After the first night camping there, it was gone. Some animal must have come for it in the night, when I was sound asleep.

"Is it still safe to camp here?" I inquired.

"Well, there haven't been any cases of human infection yet, but as a precaution we are closing down tomorrow and they will start treating the area."

She proceeded to tell me where my campsite was and I drove slowly to my site. The Lake Tahoe region was the most difficult place to secure a campsite of this entire trip. I spent a great deal of time searching online for a campground with vacancy. This was Fallen Leaf Campground at South Lake Tahoe, part of the U.S. Forest Service's Tahoe Recreation Area. This campground was large with many loops, but few campers remained. I pulled up to my site, and as the first order of business, I read the handouts about the plague. I learned it was a bacterial infection transmitted by rodents and fleas. Although it can be fatal it just starts with common flu like symptoms and can be treated successfully when detected early enough.

I knew I wouldn't be in contact with rodents. It's not in my liking to approach them, unless we are talking about an adorable golden-mantled ground squirrel posing for a picture in Bryce Canyon. Apart from that I didn't foresee rodents being a concern. But fleas, on the other hand, well, I didn't know a lot about flees except that they were insects and insects get around. So I stepped out of my car and drenched myself in deet, and then I soon forgot that the plague was even an issue. I set up my tent in the company of tall pines. In the distance between the pines I could see the snow-capped mountains of the Sierra Nevada. When camp was set up, I walked across the smooth paved campground road to a general store on the grounds. I wanted to inquire about the coin showers. I exchanged my dollars for coins, enough for me to have two complete shower cycles.

The campground shower facilities were very nice. Each shower was accessed from an outside door. Inside there was also a toilet, sink, mirror, and electrical outlets. Everything I could ask for in a bathroom was there. I was excited because it had been a week since I last showered.

When I was all clean and feeling refreshed I put on my swimsuit, tank top, and flip flops, and I walked a paved pathway through the forest about a mile to Lake Tahoe. I arrived and the place was busy. There was some sort of

open air restaurant and bar next to the water, and many
families and couples walked about and lounged on the
beach.

Lake Tahoe is refreshingly beautiful, especially after
having spent the past few days in the dry desert expanse of
Nevada. The tall pine forest led right up to the sand where
the clearest water I've ever seen lapped against the shore.
Across the twenty-two miles of shimmering blue were the
snow-capped mountains of the northern Sierra Nevada. I
never went out on a boat into Lake Tahoe but there are so
many ways to enjoy Lake Tahoe from land. You can look
down on it from an overlook of the road. There it is spread
out underneath the tree line and you can look down not just
upon it, but straight through it, getting a preview of how
deep it is. From here you can also observe all the coves and

The Pope House

inlets where the lake turns to hide and rest.

Another way to enjoy Lake Tahoe is what I was doing that evening from the sand of one of its many beaches, feeling like I'd made it to the ocean and had become a beach bum, while at the same time looking up at the snow-capped mountains feeling like a northern mountaineer.

I went out on a dock, and looking down the crystal clear water gave me a sensation I'd never quite felt before, almost a sort of dizziness. I've never been able to look straight down through a lake before, vision unobstructed, where I could see fish swimming around at different depths, and the sand and pebbles lying untouched at the bottom. I would not take someone out here who is afraid of heights, because even though you are nearly level to the water you are actually high up from the ground underneath, and you can see that so clearly. Despite the peculiar sensation, at the same time, it was miraculously beautiful. Beauty like this is not happenstance. It's created.

A final way I enjoyed Lake Tahoe was from one of the porches of the Baldwin and Pope Estates. There, just next to the trail I arrived on and set up behind the beach were these two estates, preserved as Tallac Historic Site, managed by the U.S. Forest Service. The estates contained a collection of houses built in the late 1800s and early 1900s that were the private resorts for three social elite families of the San Francisco Bay Area. All of these buildings were composed of wood fashioned in one way or another, blending this rustic north woods style with tudor elements. The estates included the large summer cottages, adorned with dark wooden shingles, and numerous guest houses and small log cabins for the tutor, groundskeepers, and servants. They were all tied together by well-kept pathways and gardens. During the day the buildings were open for tours, but I was there in the evening. They were all closed yet people were free to explore the grounds.

I sat on the porch of the main Pope cottage in a rocking chair. I looked out the frame of the porch structure through the dark pines to the bright blue of the lake and the mountains beyond. I imagined, just for a moment, that this was my house. I took it all in. Just a matter of hours ago I was in a ghost town off Highway 50 in the relentless desert sun. Now, I was sitting on the porch of a wealthy estate, in the shade of the sweet pines, looking out at a marvelous view. It was very relaxing. And it was all a pleasant surprise. I didn't know these estates of Tallac Historic Site existed, and I thought it was so novel and welcoming to be able to enjoy the elite life freely for a moment on this porch.

When the evening grew old, my wandering around Lake Tahoe for the day became complete, and my moment of an elitists life came to a screeching halt as I decided to grab a bite to eat at Taco Bell and visit the local Kmart.

Driving into Lake Tahoe on the southern end I wasn't impressed by the surrounding area. There were numerous casinos, tacky hotels, distasteful restaurants, and noisy traffic. Of course all things of the civilized world seem extra distasteful after having spent so much time out in nature in the wild expanse of the Great Basin. My first impression of the area was certainly, however, not favorable, but my campground so nicely situated with a short walk from the beach and the beautiful estates, with a stunning and relaxing view of the lake, gave me a very favorable memory of Lake Tahoe. I would return the next morning to the lake, to lay in the sun, read from my book about the West, and enjoy the beautiful view of Tallac and Taylor Creeks flowing into the Lake as silver ribbons.

This is one of those places that would have made a great National Park but commerce and private ownership moved in too quickly and much of the surrounding area was lost to commercial tourist consumption and casino tycoons, but as I discovered, the U.S. Forest Service does have a hold on these pockets of beauty around the lake, and I was very fortunate to discover one and also fortunate to leave without contracting the plague.

Given the opportunity, I would definitely go back.

The Golden Gate National Parks

"I'm here, but I'm not really sure where I am," I said going up to the counter in the visitor center for Point Reyes National Seashore.

After much back and forth I came to the conclusion that I would skip my plans to drive into San Francisco and stay in the Fisherman's Wharf Hostel. I had fun things planned on my original itinerary. I wanted to visit the Walt Disney Family Museum, Lombard Street, Japantown, as well as some other typical sites. But for some unknown reason at the time my plans did not sit well with me, and many nights I reviewed my atlas trying to figure out how I could change my plans.

Along my way across California from Lake Tahoe I connected to internet with my tablet and found the address to this visitor center for Point Reyes National Seashore. I decided I would pay a visit to the seashore, check out the nearby Muir Woods, and find a good view of the Golden Gate Bridge, but at the end of the day I would not cross over into San Francisco, instead I would proceed to Pinnacles National Park.

I followed my GPS instructions to the Bear Valley Visitor Center for Point Reyes National Seashore, and when I arrived I knew close to nothing about the layout of this park, what its features were, or how it fit into the surrounding area.

The National Park Service employee handed me the park map. She explained some sites worth checking out and gave advice on where to get the best view of the Golden Gate Bridge.

Leaving the visitor center I headed towards Point Reyes Lighthouse. The drive was scenic, through forest, and along the water of Tamales Bay, by little fishing ports and quaint small towns, and then into the rolling hills and grasslands that led up to Point Reyes itself. Eventually the road was closed, so I parked my car and went walking on the road at the cliff's edge.

Another couple was walking near to me. We exchanged small talk about the intense wind and thick fog which came over the place. Just moments earlier, a little further inland, the sky was blue and warm. But here it was cold, windy, and all mysterious-like. We could hear the ocean and smell the salt air, but the fog and mist was so thick that we couldn't see any water at all. All we could see along this road were the trees that grew on the sides, which had been so consistently blown by the wind that all of their branches had grown in one direction.

The lighthouse sat down lower than the plateau of the land, among rock cliffs on a peninsula, where the land fell sharply into the ocean somewhere below the fog. To get to it I had to walk down hundreds of stairs. Roaring sea and misty wind were whipping all around. Inside the lighthouse I found refuge and a small group on a tour with a Park Ranger. I listened in.

This place was fascinating but was by no means relaxing. It seemed that at any moment this lighthouse could fall off the cliffs edge into the sea hidden somewhere below the thick fog. I knew this was not going to happen, but it was astounding to imagine the lighthouse keeper having to live out here back in the day, so isolated from everyone else, and hidden in the fog for much of the year with the tumultuous weather all around. My attempt at imagining such a life inspired me to conjure up pieces of a story I considered writing, but I would eventually abandon that story and those ideas would become but a ghost town.

After seeing the lighthouse I drove down to the beach. It was so cold and windy that my visit was very brief. I got back in my car and drove further inland. I stopped by a small gourmet grocery store across the street from the bay where I ordered a double decker BLT and chicken salad sandwich which was absolutely monstrous and delicious. This was not the kind of store catering to tourists but seemed like a local establishment for the people who were so privileged to live nestled in these woods among the bay, cliffs, and sandy beaches.

Point Reyes

At one point in the day I came to a great overlook of the ocean. I looked down across the shoreline and could see the many cliffs and the very edge of California spilling into the Pacific. I noticed a path along the wispy wild grass. It descended down a hill among the cliffs to the water below. It was beautiful. I could see miles of beach and waves reaching for shore all over. The sun was warm and the California coast was just plain golden. I got down to the water and was climbing over rocks to get to a cove where I saw a beach. When I approached the cove I noticed something peculiar. Everyone was naked. There were maybe ten elderly, weathered, leathery, naked old men. Welcome to California! I turned around. I didn't want to see anymore. I passed some young clothed teenage boys descending while I was ascending. *Should I warn them? Nah, it'll be a surprise.*

I got back into my car and made my way to Muir Woods National Monument, named after John Muir, famous adventurer, author, and conservationist. He was alive from 1838 to 1914 and is one of the greatest and my most admired explorers. He wisely advocated for the preservation of American wilderness, back before conservation was a thing. He is informally referred to as the father of the National Parks. As a skilled writer he involved people in his adventures through essays and books. I admire John Muir greatly for his view of the world. Like myself, he looked everywhere and saw design and meaning. He viewed nothing in nature as accident but all as part of a continual creation. He also saw commonality in design throughout nature and saw unity in the entire natural world, which he writes reveals the "glorious traces of the thoughts of God."

All throughout the day, with all my driving through the Point Reyes area cars were sparse and parking was ample, but here at Muir Woods the place was full and many people were walking alongside the narrow road. These people looked like true city folk, parking in every nook and cranny. All lots had signs stating they were at capacity, but I'd come to not trust those signs. I was able to snag a spot quickly as another car was pulling out.

I was excited to go to Muir Woods because I thought I was going to Muir's home and would be able to learn more about him. I was wrong, so when I arrived at the park I was very confused. I kept looking for his house. It wasn't there. This was just a section of forest named after him. I discovered Muir Woods is basically a series of short paths and boardwalks through a Redwood forest, adorned at times with quotes of John Muir and signs asking visitors to be quiet and enjoy the scenery. This was my first experience in a Redwood forest. Although similar to Sequoias, the Redwoods seem much more jungle-like, in a wetter environment, with giant ferns and more plant life growing on the forest floor. The Sequoia seems to be much more of a dry pine and very much fits the dry-piney feel of the Sierra Nevada.

I took this visit to Muir Woods as a preview to what I would eventually find in the future in the Redwood Forest National Park. Based on just the preview from the Muir Woods I knew the Redwood Forest National Park must be amazing and inspiring.

My final stop of the day's exploration was a visit to the Golden Gate Bridge. A prime viewpoint was from a place called Battery Spencer, a nineteenth century concrete battery. There was parking at the battery, but when I was there the lot was full. There were even cars lined up waiting to pull in.

I drove further down Conzelman Road. There was another lot for people to park and observe the bridge. It too was full. I eventually found parking at a third lot, which on Google Maps is called Golden Gate Public View. Since the view at Battery Spencer was the closest and seemingly best I decided to run alongside the road .6 miles from the small parking lot to Battery Spencer. I got to enjoy the Golden Gate Bridge along my run.

Might I say the Golden Gate Bridge is something

definitely worth seeing. The immensity of the bridge, along
with the fact that it was constructed in and over water, is
nearly beyond comprehension. It is quite a view. I stood
there captivated in wonder, imagining Baymax and Hiro
from Disney's *Big Hero 6* flying up around its giant red spires
and observed the little miniature San Francisco on the other
side.

I might not have made it to San Francisco itself but
my visit to the surrounding Point Reyes National Seashore,
Muir Woods, and Golden Gate Recreational Area was definitely a rewarding experience. At Pinnacles National Park I
would soon find out that all of my hesitation to go to San
Francisco was for a reason.

When I arrived at Pinnacles it was late that night,
around 11 p.m. I had a hard time seeing campsites and ori-
enting myself to the grounds in the dark, but I eventually got
a rough grasp. I quickly popped up Kelty and found the
campground bathroom. Signs were posted everywhere about
the extreme threat of wildfire, but I wasn't too concerned.
The bathroom was located right next to the campground
host's site. My car trunk had become unorganized, so as I
was brushing my teeth and getting ready for bed I kept having to open the trunk, and this door and that door, searching
for things. I was growing concerned that I would become a
nuisance to the campground hosts, but as far as I knew they
weren't too disturbed.

Back at the campsite I zipped myself into my tent. I
had covered a lot of ground, seen a lot of sights this day,
and now it was late so I was tired and fell asleep quickly.

PINNACLES OF PURPOSE

I was venturing out of Pinnacles National Park in a land-scape that I still struggle to describe. There were trees and there were plants, but everything was extremely weary and dry. Drought and too many days like today, with 104 degrees, had taken a toll on the landscape. I was fortunate to get my hiking done very early in the morning before the sun came out to scorch. Everything around me was so thirsty. Stream beds were dried up, bridges that once passed over water passed over rock and dust, and adorning all park structures were signs warning of extreme fire danger.

Despite its conditions the park was fascinating with enormous volcanic boulders to crawl and climb under and around. Also, no one was there. The heat and threat of fire was probably enough to keep most visitors away and allow me to have the park to myself.

The plan now was to drive to Los Angeles, a seven

hour journey to the great Pacific coast and the energy of the
city. This was a change from my original plan. I had been set
on visiting San Francisco, staying in a hostel, and visiting the
Walt Disney Family Museum, but for the past four days I
had been plagued with an uncanny feeling– a strange un-
comfortableness with my plan. I would be out hiking, enjoying the captivation of nature, and then my mind would wander off to my San Francisco plan and I would begin to question if I should follow through. At night I would study my
road atlas trying to find good reason to change the course of
my journey. I really found no legitimate reason to all my hes-
itancy, and that perhaps is what troubled me the most. I had
done my research. I had made my plans and reservations.
On the surface everything was in order, but this hesitation
would not leave me. So after four days of wrestling with my
decisions I changed my plan. My reason for this was not a
very logical one but rather based seemingly on intuition. Later I would discover there was something much greater behind these feelings than my own intuition.

   Thirty miles removed from Pinnacles National Park I
still hadn't seen anything noteworthy, just the peculiar desert
-like landscape and an occasional tumbleweed, but then finally the first sign of life– a mother and what appeared to be
her daughter waving on the side of the road next to their
car. They obviously needed help, but I continued on driving.
I had a new plan to follow and I knew the trip to Los Angeles would be a long one. Then suddenly my mind was
prompted to recall my canyons and my most sprawling canyon of all: selfishness. I knew in that moment I needed to let

light into my canyon of selfishness. I needed to turn around and help these people. I felt convicted.

I turned around and drove back. I rolled down my window, and they immediately started speaking in Spanish. Not a problem. I speak Spanish. They told me that they ran out of gas. "Have you called anyone for help?" I asked. They informed me there was no phone service in the area. We were in the middle of nowhere. I had never run into this sort of situation before. *How does it work? Are they trying to trick me into something? How do I help them? Well, I guess I need to drive to the nearest town and bring them back some gas.* "I'll go and get you gas. Wait for me. I will return," I told them.

I searched my GPS for the nearest gas station and the screen displayed a forty mile distance to the nearest one. Forty miles there and forty miles back would certainly put me behind on my journey, but I knew I needed to help these people. This moment was actually a pinnacle and pivotal moment in my summer.

On my way to the nearest gas station I was overcome with the most joyous and fulfilling emotions as I put the puzzles of the past few days together. There was a reason for everything. There was a reason I was plagued with uncanny feelings about going to San Francisco. There was a reason why I changed my plan. There was a reason why I decided to head to Los Angeles instead of San Francisco. If I didn't have those feelings, if I didn't change my plans, if I wasn't on my way to Los Angeles, these people would be stranded and at the mercy of the desert in the 104 degrees. But random events and purposeless intuition were not the

reasons for all of this coming together. I knew this was orchestrated and that's what filled me with this joy. We could
say this all started weeks before in Canyonlands National
Park when God made me aware of the canyons in my own
life. Being aware of my selfishness made me more sensitive
to my actions and the need for change. The hesitation about
going to San Francisco was not solely my intuition but rather the Holy Spirit alive and at work in me, prompting me
and guiding me to this moment.

 While I could have felt burdened by my own obliga-
tion to goodwill, rather I felt extremely blessed. Because this
moment was verification for me that God had been and is
working in me. I felt so humbled yet empowered to be a
part of God's plan. I felt so purposeful.

 After my drive, which was more like a rocket ship
ride of emotions, my GPS led me to an abandoned factory
but there was a gas station in front. I pulled up to the pump
only to notice that this gas station too was part of the ghost
town. I drove a little further and rolled into a small McFar-
land-style town with a gas station and people selling tacos
on the side of the road. I went inside to the convenient
store of the gas station to explain my situation.

 They informed me that they didn't have gas cans. I
left and found an auto body shop. I filled up a gas can and
bought some water to take back to these stranded acquaintances.

 On the drive back I was at first concerned that these
people wouldn't be there and all of these feelings of purpose and pieces coming together would actually prove false,

but I came to the conclusion that this would still be very meaningful and worth my time. I knew that what I was doing was actually an act of worship. I was getting gas for God, considering him in the "least of these." I'm entertained with the thought that the high church could list fanciful things to bring before the altar of God, but I would bring my gas can to God, and it would be very meaningful.

Despite my speculation they were still there and extremely thankful when I poured gas into their car. "Muchisimas gracias," they told me. It wasn't just convenient that I could communicate to these people in Spanish. I knew this was on purpose, and there was something important I needed to communicate to them. I told them in all sincerity, "don't thank me, thank God, because He put me in your path." They agreed with me and said in Spanish, "Thanks be to God." I gave them the bottles of water. They insisted on paying me and then took off, and that was that. I stood alone in the desert next to my car with a feeling of fulfillment and a smile on my face. *Life is beautiful,* I thought.

I know these people may feel blessed to have received my help, but really I feel more blessed to have helped them, knowing that God was working through me and brought meaning and fulfillment to all my feelings and changed plans.

I share this story not to brag on anything I have done, but rather to bring glory to God. I just find it so awesome how God coordinates to provide. I also think this story serves as an example of how the Holy Spirit may work in one's life. Next time you have hesitation about something without good reason I say stop, pray, and be still. These feelings may not be plain intuition or a bothersome anxiety. Maybe these feelings are not bad at all, but rather the Holy Spirit prompting you. Listen. Just listen. Don't get caught up in your emotions but listen for purpose. Maybe God is trying to put you on the path of someone to help or is trying to help you out of your Canyon. If you haven't invited God into your life and are struggling to find purpose and meaning, it is in Him that you find it. Reach out to Him. His Spirit wills and acts in His people to fulfill His purpose and fill your life with meaning, even in the simplest of things.

EXPLORING LOS ANGELES

Los Angeles– there's a certain energy about it that's unique and always enticing. It's about more than just the beautiful beaches which lay on its outskirts, its wide boulevards outlined with palm trees, the luxury of Beverly Hills that's almost incomprehensible, and the grit and dust of the city which sprawls with seemingly unlimited people and opportunities. Los Angeles is a place that has made a name for itself, and I want to experience that name and try to figure it out. It's a hard place to figure out because its just so diverse.

Here's how I see it. It's the land of surfers and skateboarders, of Hollywood trendsetters, and the social elite. It's the land of the vain and self-obsessed, the diehard liberal, and the vegan gluten free soccer mom. It's the land of graffiti, the burrito, towering palm trees, expansive beaches, and Mexican immigrants. It's a land of new ideas and lost dreams, of success and failure, high tops and flip flops, and sprawling poverty in the dusty dry air. It's a land of struggle, of creativity, of bright neon colors… and traffic, horrible traffic.

This would be my second visit to the Los Angeles area. The summer before I visited downtown Los Angeles, Hollywood, and Disneyland for the first time while I camped in Malibu and Laguna Beach. This year I was making a last minute decision to visit Los Angeles. I was arriving from Pinnacles National Park and would stay with my friend Ricky in Huntington Beach.

I had a hard time trying to get in contact with Ricky. My backup plan was to try and find a spot to camp in Crystal Cove State Park at Laguna Beach. I had camped there before, but the only campsites that would likely be vacant were the hike-in campsites three miles removed from the beach up in the hills. Luckily contact was made and I was able to invite myself to stay at Ricky's with his welcome.

Ricky has been a long distance good friend of mine who is just a couple years older than me. He is someone I find to be very smart, of sound judgment, and also adventurous. He can talk about and entertain just about any topic, which makes him interesting. Recently he has been investing in his future by studying and training to become a pilot. Originally from Ohio, he moved to Los Angeles alone, and after being followers of each other on social media we were able to meet last summer and we hit it off. Although sometimes hard to get a hold of, when I do get a hold of him he is a good listener and always willing to help out. He advised me when I was looking to buy my car later this year, and that meant a lot to me.

Driving into Huntington Beach, traffic was horrendous. Traffic all throughout the greater L.A. region is always bad, but an accident had three lanes of traffic reduced to one. When I arrived Ricky had to do some grocery shopping. I accompanied him and was excited to finally, after nearly a month, buy some cereal and milk, something that was typically a staple in my diet. Something that is usually so commonplace was now exciting.

Ricky owned a nice condominium which he was constantly renovating, with plans to increase its value, sell it, and move out of California. He had a guest room where he blew up a giant air mattress for me. I felt like I was living the life of luxury. I had a comfortable and spacious mattress to sleep on, running water just steps away, and access to a hot shower and a bowl of cereal and milk! That evening we caught up a little and I inquired about places to visit in the city. I'd be here for two days. I wanted to spend the second at Disneyland, but I needed some recommendations for the first. Ricky had to work but he provided some good recommendations, and we planned on meeting up at the end of the following day for dinner.

Ricky gave me a key to his condo so I could come and go as I pleased. The next morning I was up bright and early. My first stop of the day was the Old Los Angeles Zoo in Griffith Park. Griffith Park is a massive park in Los Angeles that houses many different features and trails. The zoo that was once there was abandoned as a new zoo was constructed elsewhere in the park. Now the abandoned zoo cages and walkways can be explored. One can even go right inside the areas the animals used to dwell in. I climbed into one area and took this picture and posted it online with this caption:

"Visit the old Los Angeles zoo and see the wild Josh in captivity. The Josh is a very adaptable amiable creature who can be found in prairies, temperate forests, alpine tundra, and dry deserts. The Josh is native to North America but it is believed to be an ancestor of those from the Iberian peninsula. The Josh is an omnivore and gatherer whose diet consists of meats, vegetables, nuts and berries, breakfast cereals, and tacos. When threatened the Josh is known to retreat and is rarely found to be aggressive. "

Leaving the Old Zoo, I proceeded to the top of the park where the Griffith Observatory lies. I was there early enough that the place was very quiet. The observatory building itself is a beautiful white domed deco style planetarium, with an astronomers monument and sundial out front. It appears in many movies.

I wasn't so much interested in that building as I was in the view of the Hollywood sign and L.A. down below in the distance from atop that hill. The view of the Hollywood sign was clear but the hazy dusty and polluted sky made Los Angeles difficult to see. Also from the observatory a series of dusty trails ran down the hill. I was familiar with these trails because a lot of celebrities and YouTubers from the area love to take pictures and videos from this place. I literally ran down a trail, for time's sake, because there was much more to see. I wanted to experience it, but I didn't want to spend a lot of time here. Running back up the sandy path was a very strenuous workout. When I got back to my car I turned the air conditioning on full. The parking lot had grown crowded. I connected to the parking-lot's wifi network to determine my next move.

I ended up at the Autry Museum of the American West located right on the corner of Griffith Park. I had driven by it earlier and it looked interesting. Parking at the museum was ample and easy and so I decided to give it a go. When I got inside I was fully enthralled. I had spent many nights of this trip reading my book about the American West as I traveled through the West. Paring that book and this whole trip together, made history come to life for me.

And this museum was the grand finale. Numerous things I had read and learned about were now before my eyes. The museum told the history of the West and was filled with relics from the era of the cowboys, natives, and pioneers. There was one room with fancy old bars and slot machines taken out of saloons. Another was filled with old sheriff badges and elaborately designed revolvers that were fine pieces of art. There were also artifacts from the native people, a California stagecoach, paintings depicting many scenes and landscapes, sculptures of characters of the West, and a whole exhibit dedicated to the singing cowboy era of Hollywood. As a grand finale I came to a room with a complete chuck wagon. As silly as it may sound I was so excited by the chuck wagon. I read so much about it in my book and now I was seeing one before me with every part explained. It made the strenuous life of the cowboy all the more real to me.

Leaving the museum I was very satisfied. I stopped at a Del Taco near the park for a quick lunch and then I drove to the Glendale Transportation Center, which serves as an Amtrak station. I admired its Mission Revival and Spanish Colonial Revival Style architecture. I then searched my GPS for a place to get a haircut, because I needed one, and I wanted to look good and on point for all my pictures with Disney characters the following day, truth be told. My attempt to find a barber was unsuccessful, but I ended up at the Goodwill Southern California Outlet. It was huge and on the edge of Hollywood. My thrifty mind knows that a Goodwill store is only as good as the wealth which surrounds it. Sure enough I found a great find– a pair of Nike high-tops, which looked like they stepped right out of the 90s untouched, with bright green zig-zag stripes on the sides, purple heels, and orange paint artistically splattered on the sides. This had to be my best thrift store find to date.

While I was standing in line a middle aged Latina woman, with her hands full of clothes, started talking to me."Those are *muy bien lindos*," she said. "Make sure you take good care of them. Get the green soap they sell at the laundromat. That works really well on shoes to keep them clean."

"Oh, is that right?" I had to say something.

"Yes, use the green soap. It comes in the little packet. It's like a miracle on shoes. They sell it for like twenty-five cents. You know what I'm talking about right?"

I nodded my head to pacify her enthusiasm. I loved how she assumed I knew what her laundromat was and the soap they sold there. *Thanks for assuming I'm a local. That's flattering,* I thought, *but I know nothing about your laundromat and their soap.*

I thanked her and walked out of there having bought the best L.A. souvenir I could never have imagined.

My final stop was at Downtown Disney where I would purchase my Disneyland ticket for the following day. Downtown Disney at Disneyland is a very chill place, especially in comparison to Disney World. You can just sort of walk around leisurely in Downtown Disney in and out different stores and around restaurants, enjoying the bright colors and tasteful instrumental Disney music playing in the background. I grabbed a sandwich at Earl of Sandwich and then went into the World of Disney store, where I bought a Mickey Mouse tank top I would wear into the park the following day. I may not have gotten my haircut, but I got a pair of sweet kicks and a cool Mickey tank. I was gonna be a cool cat walking around the park.

Once I was back at Ricky's, we went to a casual Peruvian restaurant located in a nearby strip mall for dinner. Over some lomo saltado we opened up to each other about our love interests. I told Ricky about a young lady I worked very close with whom I found really attractive and felt very hopeful with. She shared so many interests with me, was smart and with it, and seemed to have a similar upbringing. I admired her intelligence, her sense of adventure, her humor, her simple style, and most attractive of all, her interactions with others. My plan was to ask her out once I was back home. I was so excited about the prospect that during this trip, there were multiple occasions I would be driving, thinking about her, and in all the excitement of imagining a life together, my heart would start beating faster, and I would find myself going ninety miles per hour. I had to slow down.

Unfortunately, when the summer was over and the time had come to pursue her. She dismissed me, showing no interest. I had to move on, and so I suppose somewhere, amongst my grand map of life, there is a little ghost town with her name across it.

After our Peruvian food, Ricky drove me to another strip mall (It seems everything in the L.A. area is in a strip mall) where we had some ice cream. I had some Frosted Flakes flavored ice cream. Ricky talked to me about Instagram and this social media strategy he had. He asked me if I had a social media strategy. I had never even heard that term before. We proceeded deeper into the topic of the internet, and I asked him about where data on the internet is stored. He explained it in great detail.

Back at the condo, when we were both wrapping up the day getting ready for bed, I was working on a strategy, not a social media strategy, but a Disneyland strategy. One should not walk into a Disney park without a strategy. A Disneyland strategy takes some fine skill and careful consideration. I plugged in my camera to charge, laid out my outfit for tomorrow, and secured my park ticket, which prominently displayed Olaf's face on it, in my wallet. I was ready, Disneyland, here I come!

DISNEYLAND NATIONAL PARK?

"Disneyland is pretty much a National Park, right?" asked the tour guide at the Walt Disney Studios in Burbank, California. It was the summer before and I was fortunate enough to be able to tour the production studio. The guide asked me what I was doing in California all the way from Kentucky. I explained that I was on a National Park trip. He lumped Disneyland in with the likes of Yosemite, Death Valley, and Sequoia as I was explaining where I had already been.

Disneyland, in my eyes, is a National Historic Site. Such a place was revolutionary at the time of its creation—a theme park which encompasses the best of the American spirit. It was a dream come true from a man who started life in the humblest of means in Missouri, who created the most influential business the entertainment industry. Walt Disney himself, at the opening of the park in 1955 said, "To all who come to this happy place; welcome. Disneyland is your land. Here age relives fond memories of the past...and here youth may savor the challenge and promise of the future. Disneyland is dedicated to the ideals, the dreams and the hard facts that have created America...with the hope that it will be a source of joy and inspiration to all the world."

I believe it is just that. At least for me it is. I learned that in Disneyland's early years foreign dignitaries would often make one of their first stops in the United States to Disneyland for a condensed crash course on American culture and history, one that of course is rosified by Disney's idealistic fashion. But here in Disneyland you can walk down a quintessential Midwest main street, visit the American frontier, stroll down New Orleans Square, board the Mark Twain Riverboat, visit Tom Sawyer Island, immerse yourself in fairy tales we have adopted as a culture, and board a train and ride through the diverse landscapes as if traveling across the nation. Nowhere else in the world would a man, not born into a family of power nor influence, be allowed the freedom and opportunity to build not only Disneyland but accomplish what Walt Disney did during his lifetime. Disneyland encapsulates the potential there is within this great nation for those who dream big.

When I approach Disneyland I don't come to it simply for frill and fancy, but I come to it with all the knowledge I have learned about Walt Disney and the history that was created in the making of this place. Taking into account its rich history and what it meant when it was first opened makes the place all the more interesting. I tour Disneyland not just as theme park but as a living museum and tribute to America.

I'd been to both Disneyland and Disney World before. Disney World in Florida is very grandiose. Seeing Cinderella's castle can fill the true Disney fans which fanciful emotion, and one could spend a week or more exploring Disney World. Disneyland has an entirely different feel about it. One can stand before Sleeping Beauty's castle, and instead of being swept away in awe think, *aww, that's cute.* Everything in the park is kind of miniature and very whimsical, like a small scale Disney World, but it's the original— the true vision of Walt Disney, and that is what makes it special.

The Disneyland park employee scanned my ticket and I turned the turnstile. Immediately I was transported into the idealistic world of Walt Disney. To my left was the fire station, where Walt himself used to have an apartment. I rushed down Main Street U.S.A. to the Hub. The Hub is the central circle of the park where the statue of Walt and Mickey is in front of the castle and where pathways lead into all of the various lands of Disneyland, like spokes on a bicycle. All of the access paths were roped off, and people crowded into the Hub, waiting for the rest of the park to open. I had arrived early, as one must do if they want to get on all his or her choice rides and pack the day full. I stood there with anxious anticipation. Music from Disney Pixar's film, *Up,* played in the background. I was ready. I had a plan.

This summer was Disneyland's "Season of the Force," and so there were various rides, shows, and events created in celebration of *Star Wars: The Force Awakens* having been released in December and Disney now owning Lucasfilm. I wanted to visit the new rendition of Space Mountain renamed Hyperspace Mountain. Secondly I wanted to visit Star Wars Launch Bay, a Star Wars museum and location in which one can meet and take photos with Star Wars characters. My Plan after these few things was much more relaxed. I had been on most attractions in the park from my visit the previous year so I thought this time I wanted to take things easy, embrace the scenery, notice the fine details, and admire the park for it's design.

I was never a fan of Space Mountain. Riding around in the dark, not knowing what turn the coaster is going to make, leaves my body feeling like it's flailing around. And as a tall person, it seems at times as if my head is going to be chopped off from the track above and the metal framework inside. Although I know that there is truly no danger involved, it makes for an uncomfortable ride. Hyperspace Mountain was no different. There were occasional projections throughout with clips of Star Wars space crafts and Star Wars music playing to add to the thrill, but Hyperspace Mountains was a little "Hyped" up.

With my curiosity appeased I proceeded to Star Wars Launch Bay. I quickly swept through the museum, seeing some props and droid shells used in the movies. I held the excitement of a seven year old to meet my favorite wookie, Chewbacca. The line was short and as I approached the hairy beast he gave me a big wookie hug.

Next I found myself waiting to see Kylo Ren. In line,

on display, were showcases of all the Jedi and Sith Lightsabers. This section of the museum had an Imperial theme. The ominous march theme of the Empire filled the corridor which was modeled after the hallways of a star destroyer or the Death Star. In all sincerity I was a little on edge, filled with nervous anticipation. I was about to Meet Kylo Ren, this irrational, angsty, unhinged wheeler of the dark side of the Force and I had nothing to defend myself. Okay, I know he wasn't real, but they say Disneyland appeals to the kid in everyone and here I was like a child, my imagination on fire.

As I came closer and closer to the front of the line the more this fluttery anticipation stirred within me. What would I say to Kylo Ren? How would I respond if he asked me to join the First Order? All I wanted was a picture. How do you ask Kylo Ren to take a picture? Obviously he has more important things to do like oppressing the poor, destroying planets, killing Jedi's, being emo, listening to gothic punk, hating his family, feeling sorry for himself, and wreaking havoc on the galaxy. I mean, let's be real, Kylo Ren doesn't care for taking a selfie with me.

Then the Disneyland employee motioned me forward. It was my turn. I tried to shake off the nervousness, but I was led down a quiet hallway and eeriness was ever present. Then around from the corner slowly appeared the emotionless dark mask of the villain. "Come" he said motioning me into a room clearly staged for photos.

He did ask me to join the First Order, in his mechanical tone through his faceless and impersonal mask. I don't remember how I responded. I just wanted a photo. Let's take it and get me out of here, I thought. And so we did.

Phew!

I know it wasn't real, but kudos to Disney for making this experience believable in the moment.

Unfortunately I didn't like how the photos turned out, so I decided to experience the whole thing again later in the day, for a second chance at a good photo.

After the first try I decided to take it easy and enjoy some breakfast on Main Street at the Jolly Holiday Bakery and Cafe. I ordered a coffee and a quiche with a side of fruit, and sat outside on the patio and enjoyed just being in Disneyland.

Next I hit up all the old Fantasyland rides. There's Pinocchio's Daring Adventure, Snow White's Scary Adventures, Alice in Wonderland, Peter Pan's Flight, and Mr. Toad's Wild Ride. They are my favorite part of Disneyland because they are such old rides and Disneyland originals. Some were there at the opening of the park and were not something added on to pander to the modern audience. Getting on them is truly a classic Disney experience, an authentic look into Walt's vision. The Pinocchio and Snow White rides are like riding through an antique attraction, but in a tasteful and appealing sort of way.

My Disney World and Disneyland strategy has always been to hit up these Fantasyland rides early in the morning because they aren't the rides people rush to, but the lines do grow long later in the day. Most people rush to the more thrilling rides early in the day. I avoid those lines and go on those top attractions during meal hours.

Since I had been to Disneyland before I wasn't anxious about seeing it all, but there were some staples I had to visit including Splash Mountain, It's a Small World, The Haunted Mansion, Indiana Jones Adventure, Thunder Mountain Railroad, and Pirates of the Caribbean.

Some of these rides are found in Disney World but in Disneyland they are a bit different. I particularly prefer Disneyland's Pirates of the Caribbean over Disney World's version. It's much longer and starts off passing by a restaurant, entering into a swamp, setting the swashbuckling mood, and easing the passengers into the rest of the voyage; And It's a Small World, though smaller than Disney World's is the original from the 1964 World's Fair, and careful eyes can see various Disney characters added within the ride, including Woody, Jessie, Bullseye, Lilo, Stitch, Ariel, and Aladdin.

I wanted to end my visit to Disneyland with a ride aboard the P.J. Railroad, but it was closed due to construction of the new Star Wars land. So after my stay in the park, I proceeded to Disney's California Adventure. This is the adjoining Disney park next to Disneyland. I had purchased a multi-park ticket so was able to scan into the other park.

I'm a huge fan of Disney's California Adventure. It's a California themed park. There's a re-creation of Hollywood Boulevard; Paradise Peer (recently renamed Pixar Pier), supposedly modeled after Santa Monica Pier; Cars Land, embracing the rural desert stretches of the state; and Grizzly Peaks, a National Forest and Sierra Nevada-esque themed part of the park, with river rapids and outdoor attractions.

Cars Land is my favorite of all Disney attractions. It's a physical rendition of Radiator Springs from the movies, and it's a very immersive experience. It includes Radiator Springs Racers– a ride in which the passenger embarks in one of the cars from the movies, rides through the highlights of the original *Cars* movie, and ends with a race against fellow car riders through the recreated California desert. It's a thrill and the animatronic cars are very mesmerizing. It's one of the most popular attractions in the park and therefore very busy, but Disneyland has single rider lines, where they group in solo park visitors into rides when single seats are available. Those lines usually shrink very fast. So I've gotten on Radiator Springs Racers twice with ease.

Elsewhere in Disney's California Adventure the Frozen Broadway musical was premiering. Lines to get in the theater were ridiculously long. They could have stretched all the way from Arendale to Oaken's Trading Post and Sauna, but I had gotten in line forty minutes before doors opened. The summer before, and previous years the theater held the abbreviated version of the Broadway musical Aladdin, but just like Jafar getting trapped in a magic genie lamp, Disney packed up that production, let it go, and opened up the gate to the Frozen production. It was a well put together show, and as much as Frozen has kind of oversaturated culture, and I sometimes wish Olaf would just melt in the California heat, I am glad I was able to see it. It was great, *Hans-down*.

Later I visited some staple attractions in Disney's

California Adventure including Ariel's Undersea Adventure, Mike and Sully to the Rescue, and Toy Story Midway Mania. I then took a pause in Grizzly Peak to eat at Smoke-jumpers Grill, ordering a grilled chicken sandwich and piling on mounds of toppings at the self-serve bar. Nearby I met Pluto and took a picture with him.

After dinner I went back over to Disneyland and walked around the stores of Main Street U.S.A.. Sunset was approaching and that's when all the locals and season pass holders pile into the park for the evening Main Street Electrical Parade and fireworks. I had seen them both before, and didn't want to deal with the oppressive crowds so I left satisfied with my Disneyland experience.

Disneyland paints fond memories in my mind and it truly is an exciting experience. I believe I will always be a fan of Disneyland and will welcome any opportunity to visit again, but I particularly remember during this visit that the excitement and appeal of Disneyland is diminished greatly after visiting the natural marvels of the U.S. National Parks. Nature itself provides attractions that far outperform Disneyland's in magic appeal. Walt Disney himself said:

"Landscapes of great wonder and beauty lie under our feet and all around us. They are discovered in tunnels in the ground, the heart of flowers, the hollows of trees, fresh-water ponds, seaweed jungles between tides, and even drops of water. Life in these hidden worlds is more startling in reality than anything we can imagine."

Sea Foam and Seals

Crystal Cove State Park in California. I found it in a magazine. The picture alone was the selling point. I had been here the summer before when I camped three miles up in the hills and bluffs alongside the ocean. Up there, remotely camping, with the ocean ahead and below on one side and the glow of Los Angeles in the distance behind me was a truly unique camping experience. I was in a super busy area of the country but found a secret area of peace and solitude.

This summer I was back at Crystal Cove just for the day. I had left Ricky's home in the morning when he left for work. Today I needed to make my way towards Las Vegas where I would fly the next morning back to Chicago. Ricky had recommended that I save my drive for later in the evening, because if I tried during the day the roads would be ridiculously busy with Fourth of July weekend traffic.

I started talking to someone at Crystal Cove who also recommended I leave later, so I decided just to make a day

of it at Crystal Cove. Although the campsites right next to
the beach are very popular, the beach at Crystal Cove is not.
The park is located in Laguna Beach and so people chose
the more popular beach named after the town. That's where
all the action is. Here it's a little quieter. Crystal Cove has a
series of trails in the hills and bluffs, the beach, and the
camping. It's all accessible from one main parking lot. It's a
very clear and well managed state park.

When I pulled into the lot I parked my car at the far
end where it was quiet and still, where I could be free to
spread out, because my first order of business was to clean
out my car and pack up. I had lived a month out of this car.
I had things tucked in every nook and cranny. I had camping supplies, souvenirs, food, sand, and all sorts of odds and
ends I had accumulated.

I pulled out my suitcases and spread them open in
the parking lot. I opened all four doors of the vehicle and I
began to organize. I thought the whole scene looked ridiculous as I was so spread out.

As I pulled out my pins and stickers for Capitol Reef
and Arches I began to get sentimental. It seemed so long
ago yet it was all on the same trip. I had traveled so far and
seen so many things. I tried brushing the red Utah sand out
of the car, which had accumulated around the driver's seat. I
gathered up all my park maps from Saguaro all the way to
Great Basin and secured them together in a bag from Disneyland. I had my Rocky Mountain tie-dye t-shirt, my sweet
L.A. kicks, the flyer on the plague from Lake Tahoe— I figured I could toss that. I found my map of Nevada with the

ghost towns highlights by the park ranger —I wanted to keep that. I had two SD memory cards full of photos, a tin cup from the general store in Moab so I could cook oatmeal over the fire, and my journal with pages exploring my thoughts on the Canyonlands.

There were so many pieces of my adventure to pack up, and it was all so meaningful. Everything held a story and I felt very accomplished and fortunate. I had completed the journey, and I had grown in many ways. I could say I grew in experience while also growing in understanding of myself, life, my canyons, and the world around me. Along with that my imagination grew, having visited many different environments and landscapes I had never before experienced, my ability to reimagine, revisit, and wander around these places in my mind would now be in my capacity.

When I was done packing up everything I put on my flip flops and swimming trunks and headed down the short sandy path to the beach. Crystal Cove is named appropriately. The beach is located in a cove and to me crystal is congruent with the beauty this place presents. Some think crystal as clear. The water is nice but not clear as crystal. To me crystal also seems delicate and fine, almost like a gem, and this place is a gem. Its fine and exquisite in beauty– blue sky, blue ocean, sandy beach, sharp rocks with the waves dancing dramatically upon them. I took in the deep salty air, drug my toes into the sand, listened to old man ocean endlessly speak. I layed down and felt the salty breeze blow across my skin and the sun surround me in warmth.

After resting there a while the sky grew cloudy and

the air brisk. The wind caused beautiful waves to crash into rocks extra tall and crescendo into the air on the sides of the beach. I went for a walk and saw something dark pop out of the water a short distance off and remain. It was a seal swimming toward land in the foamy sea.

Out in the distance above the water light beams broke through the clouds sending spotlights down upon the ocean, reminiscent of the beams shooting into the dark crevices of the Canyonlands and illuminating the mountains peaks in the Rocky Mountains. They served as a reminder of what I had learned throughout this trip, how God desires to illuminate the dark places in our lives, make them beautiful, and take us out of our canyons leading us to the mountain tops, where we find fulfillment and peace.

The ocean, the way it roars, the way it endlessly speaks, the way it crashes, soothes, refreshes, evokes feeling, and is always moving is a reminder of the life God has breathed into the world. Not only that, but the ever present waves remind us of the ever constant presence of God in all of nature. God I believe is the author of movement—to feel the breeze and hear the ocean is to feel the movement of God.

When the wind grew even stronger and the air cooler I decided to return to my car and begin the final step of my summer adventure. The plan was to drive to Red Rock Canyon National Conservation Area just outside of Las Vegas, camp, and then wake up early for my flight back to Chicago. There however would be a few unexpected occurrences that would add just a little more story to be told.

Flying into Space

Before me, out my windshield, I could see the pavement end. A belt of asteroids floated in dark space. There was no way I could have expected this. I was searching for my campground, couldn't find it, and now I had reached Earth's edge. I had no clue what to do, and there was no time to consider how to handle the situation. I'd have fly out into space in my Hyundai Accent.

How did I get here? Last point of major interest was earlier in the day at Crystal Cove State Park in Laguna Beach, California. I had spent the day there beside the beach, organizing my car and trying to avoid the holiday weekend traffic I'd encounter mid day between Los Angeles and Las Vegas. The following day I was to fly out of Las Vegas back to Chicago, ending my great summer adventure out West. This night I had plans to camp in Red Rock Canyon National Recreation Area right on the outskirts of Las Vegas.

The highway had been busy but there was no sitting in traffic. The drive took about six hours and I arrived at around 11 p.m.. Along the way a major rain storm set in. I welcomed it, because my rental car was plastered with dry dirt from all over the West and I'd feel much better about turning it in if one could actually see the blue paint instead of the plastered dirt and sand.

When it rains in the desert it pours. It was fiercely and thoroughly cleaning off my car. I could almost feel the weight of the rain as it pounded against the windshield. The wipers couldn't keep up, but the road was straight and level and I could manage. Between bouts of rain I would see the bright flashing lights of the casino resorts on the outskirts of Las Vegas. Thousands of flashing light bulbs decorated these signs, and I wondered what kind of people stay in these huge casino resorts.

At one point, still in California, I stopped at a McDonalds for a chicken sandwich. I asked for a cup of water. The employee told me that a cup of water will cost the same as a cup of soda. I found it very usual. In the East and Midwest water is usually free. But that's the California drought for you. I hoped this rain storm I was experiencing in Nevada stretched over to California!

To get to the Red Rock Canyon area I was following GPS coordinates. I was very tired and anxious to set up my tent set and spread out. I hadn't reserved a site because I figured not many people would be camping in the desert outside Las Vegas this time of year. Arriving very late at campgrounds is never preferred to me. I am very conscious

of the noise I make while setting up camp and getting myself together at night. I'm usually concerned I'll bother a
neighbor or wake someone up.

　　As I was approaching I was getting very sleepy. I felt
I had to turn the music up loud and turn the air conditioning onto full force to provide some stimulus to keep me
awake. It had been a long day, lots of traveling, and I was
drained. The GPS sounded "You have reached your destination," except there was nothing there. At least I didn't notice. I kept driving hoping to find a sign for a campground.
Nothing. I had no maps to the area, and it was very dark out
with no lights. Why is this happening to me? I just wanted
to sleep. I continued on for maybe twenty miles out in the
dark desert. Because it had just rained the black top was very
shiny, my headlights reflecting out on it making it glisten.
Then suddenly it seemed as if the blacktop ended and I was
approaching a field of asteroids. Three was no time to slow
down. I had been going too fast. I had to engage whatever
this was. My heart was racing. I was uncertain of what was
before me. Then I felt it. The car shook violently. Rocks
loudly broke and flew off my tires hitting underneath my
car.

　　I had to put it all together. The downpour had created a flash flood, which had ripped through the area, eroding
a hillside, bringing fragments of rock spilling onto the road
and covering it. While I was driving the rocks were still spilling, moving, creating the illusion that the road ended and
asteroids were floating through space. I thought most certainly my car would be left with considerable damage.

When the car again hit the smooth shiny black asphalt I was relieved. I was again traveling, smoothly, easily, noiseless. I pulled the car over to inspect it. It had survived without any damage.

This night continued on with a series of unfortunate events. I ran into other segments of pavement with rocks washed onto them. After venturing further into the desert expanse I returned again to my GPS coordinates of the supposed campground to take a second look. Nearby I found a turn off to a road that had a gate closed and locked. I read a sign stating it was closed due to flooding. I figured the campground must have been down there. So I officially gave up.

I had read online before that Walmart lets people sleep in their vehicles in their parking lots, so I programmed by GPS to guide me to the nearest Walmart. I was guided into Las Vegas. There was a Walmart, a Planet Fitness, Lowes, and a whole outdoor mall. I drove a few laps around the parking lot until I settled on one spot relatively in the middle, as to not stick out too bad. After I went inside to buy some water, I opened my trunk, and pulled out a sleeping bag. I wanted to cover myself completely and not appear so noticeably in my vehicle, if anyone were to pass by. Also the lights of the parking lot were very bright and I needed to block them out.

Just as I was getting situated I noticed a vehicle labeled "Security" driving around the parking lot. Something told me this plan just wouldn't work. I didn't want to be asked to leave. I'd much rather avoid that encounter, so I left.

Now I could have sought out a hotel but it was so late and I had to get up so early that it just wasn't worth the money. On top of that, I didn't know where in Las Vegas to stay. What can I afford? What is sketchy? What is safe? I didn't know. So, I did the only thing I knew to do. I drove another two hours to Valley of Fire State Park.

I had been there the previous summer a few hours before driving into Las Vegas to fly out at the end of that trip. It's an exceptionally fascinating and beautiful area full of interesting bright red rock formations. I didn't care so much for the beauty right now as I did for a place to sleep, and I knew they had a campground.

By the time I arrived I had one hour to sleep before I needed to drive back to Las Vegas to the airport. I set an alarm on my phone and seemingly after having just blinked, I had to get up. When I opened my car door I was greeted with the rich smell of the desert after the rain. I located the nearby trash can. It was a traditional trash can, one you might expect Oscar the Grouch to pop his head out of. I had to get rid of a few things. My pillow and sleeping bag were not coming with me, and I didn't have time to search out a place to donate them. So I stuffed them into the campground trash can, filling it completely. I then left.

When I got to the airport I was running short on time. I had just two hours to work with. They were doing construction on a road leading to the rental vehicle returns, so that set me back a bit. I was half expecting to get repri-manded and met with a fee, because early on in my trip I noticed, just underneath the front passenger car door, the remainder trim of the vehicle had been damaged. Paint had been scrapped off, leaving a rusty brown color. However, when the Alamo Car Rental employee walked around the vehicle to inspect it, he said nothing.

When I stepped inside the airport doors to stand in line to check in and check my luggage the line wrapped around nearly to the door. I stood there for an hour and realized I probably wouldn't make my flight. They had one attendant working for hundreds of customers in line. Then suddenly a voice started motioning us to start checking in outside the airport at a kiosk. The voice was so commanding in its instructions that I thought I should listen. So I took off for the outside. Being so tired my mind wasn't in the right place and I completely abandoned one of my two suitcases. As I approached the gliding doors someone called out "Josh." A couple I had been talking to while in line had read the tag on my suitcase. Feeling very embarrassed I went back for my bag, and then I waited, and waited, and waited outside.

The two hours had passed. My flight was gone. I went up to the counter and was reprimanded by the personnel for not checking into my flight earlier via a smartphone. First off I don't own a smartphone, and even if I did it wouldn't have made a difference. I would still have been waiting two hours in line to check my luggage. The lesson learned is that I should have arrived perhaps three to four hours before my scheduled flight. The Delta service employee made me pay a rebooking fee, giving me several hours before my flight to wind down.

I was able to leisurely make my way through the security checkpoint into the terminal. When you arrive in the Las Vegas airport there in a grand atrium with a tall escalator that takes you up to an upper level where many of the gates are. I found my gate and was at ease. Although extremely tired I felt functional. I got some food and went to a quiet area with tables next to the escalators. I figured some numbers from my past month of adventure which I posted online:

6142 - miles driven
116.2 - miles hiked
60 - Cliff Bars consumed
17 - National Parks visited
14 - number of times I pitched a tent
6 - showers taken
5 - number of times I climbed up somewhere really high and didn't know how to get back down.

Giving myself plenty of time I returned back to my gate. I was going over photos of my journey and became oblivious to the fact that they changed gates for my flight, and sadly, perhaps somewhat embarrassingly so, I missed my second flight. When I realized this and reached the new gate a few people there, who had also missed a flight, said "You must be Joshua. They kept calling your name." First I abandoned a suitcase, now I missed a second flight. I was starting to feel inept. But this is what happens to me when seriously lacking sleep.

I then was put on standby for the next available

flight to Chicago. I spent the entirety of the day and evening in the airport and ended up flying in the early a.m..

THE END OF A JOURNEY

When I finally arrived back in Chicago I was completely exhausted. Not only did I have to adjust to the three hour time change, but I also had to recover from one hour of sleep in a twenty-four hour time period. I may have come back from my trip reinvigorated, inspired, rejuvenated, refreshed, while at the same time exhausted

My dad was there to pick me up at the airport. Not saying too much, and saving my stories of adventure for later when I was more awake, I thought about how it would be a major adjustment to stay put in one place consecutive days in a row. Each day would not be filled with wild wonder and amazing scenery. It would be difficult assimilating back into ordinary life, but at the same time I thought about how taking a shower didn't have to be a huge ordeal, how I could walk a few steps and running water would flow endlessly. I also thought about how I could also open a refrigerator and food would be there. I didn't have to seek it out, and each night I could have my bed already set up for me. I didn't have to empty my lungs into a air mattress or set up a tent. And the wilderness, the beauty I saw and experienced around me, was now inside me. It was a part of my memory and an imprint in my soul that would continue to grow and inspire me. On the remainder of the car ride to my parents' house in DeKalb, Illinois I was asleep.

I would spend a week with my parents in DeKalb, and at the end of July my family would go on a vacation to Acadia National Park in Maine and stay in a lovely house nestled in the woods. When August came around I returned to Kentucky and started my sixth year of teaching Spanish with a renewed spirit. I held most of these stories of adventure inside me, as many were too busy to listen to what I had to say, but little by little they escaped from me in writing, and as the reader thank you for traveling with me and letting me be your guide.

When we arrived in DeKalb from the airport, I dragged myself in. My parents had moved to a different house while I was gone. My dad accepted a full time pastoring job with the church he had been an interim at. This change entailed my parents moving into the parsonage. With little time to make my acquaintance, I made for a bed. I noticed postcards I sent my parents from Bryce Canyon and Arches hanging on their refrigerator door as I made my way to a bedroom. My heart was struck with an emotion. What an amazing past month I had. I could hardly believe I had been to these wonderful places. My life is rich, I thought, very rich.

Some people in this world are on a quest for money, status, or power. Although those things are natural in our human condition, I'd much rather spend my time seeking beauty in the wild, collecting up experiences, and reaching greater depths of understanding of the world around me and myself.

This trip had been all of those things to me—Beauty, from the dignified stature the Saguaro to the crashing foaming waves at Crystal Cove. Experiences, from getting lost in the Rockies, summiting majestic peaks, to taking in scenery never before known to me. Understanding, from that of my country, the native cultures, Mormon pioneers, spirited cowboys, hopeful miners, and rowdy outlaws, to that which is most important, a deeper understanding of myself, the canyons that run deep that need to be illuminated, the goals in life which peak high in the sky, and the unwavering essence I want to exude.

I treasure these moments, these experiences, and all these accounts are some of my greatest riches. I revisit these landscapes time and again in my memory. They have expanded my mind and given me knew places to ponder and wander. When I look over my photos, retell these stories, and consider all I have seen and experienced I truly feel very rich, like I've found things and have had experiences that many overlook. But this richness of life is there to be shared by all. You've just got to get outside, climb a mountain, watch a sunset, listen to the forest speak and the ocean roar. Beauty is all around us and it speaks to us in terms deeper and more profound than the words of any man.

I believe this natural beauty is designed to teach and reveal God's artistry to the human soul, and when we humble ourselves to accept the wild as an artistic masterpiece, it gives us greater appreciation and empathy for it. And as we observe the wild natural beauty and wait for the voice of God to speak through it we can also consider that just as great as the beauty around us is, so too, is the beauty of a life well lived.

So, traverse your canyonlands; climb your mountain; every once in a while look back to see how far you have come, and live free and wild!

ACKNOWLEDGEMENTS

Sincere thanks goes out to my parents Michael and Amy Hodge for exposing me to the joys of nature as a young child, teaching me to write, and being supportive of my adventures. Special thanks to my mother for helping me edit this work. Thanks to my blog followers who have encouraged me and particularly to the one and only Susan Melcher whose life is an adventure. Thanks to fellow traveler, friend, encourager and colleague Jamie Hamblin who understands. Thanks to my companions on this adventure who made it all the more special including Dom, Ricky, Aunt Mary; and my cousins Paul, Ines, and Jonathan.